I0438638

Analysis of the Deconstruction of Dyke Marsh, George Washington Memorial Parkway, Virginia: Progression, Geologic and Manmade Causes, and Effective Restoration Scenarios

By Ronald J. Litwin, Joseph P. Smoot, Milan J. Pavich, Helaine W. Markewich, Erik Oberg, Ben Helwig, Brent Steury, Vincent L. Santucci, Nancy J. Durika, Nancy B. Rybicki, Katharina M. Engelhardt, Geoffrey Sanders, Stacey Verardo, Andrew J. Elmore, and Joseph Gilmer

Prepared in cooperation with the National Park Service

Open-File Report 2010–1269

U.S. Department of the Interior
U.S. Geological Survey

U.S. Department of the Interior
KEN SALAZAR, Secretary

U.S. Geological Survey
Marcia K. McNutt, Director

U.S. Geological Survey, Reston, Virginia: 2011

For more information on the USGS—the Federal source for science about the Earth, its natural and living resources, natural hazards, and the environment, visit http://www.usgs.gov or call 1-888-ASK-USGS

For an overview of USGS information products, including maps, imagery, and publications, visit http://www.usgs.gov/pubprod

To order this and other USGS information products, visit http://store.usgs.gov

Suggested citation:
Litwin, R.J., Smoot, J.P., Pavich, M.J., Markewich, H.W., Oberg, Erik, Helwig, Ben, Steury, Brent, Santucci, V.L., Durika, N.J., Rybicki, N.B., Engelhardt, K.M., Sanders, Geoffrey, Verardo, Stacey, Elmore, A.J., and Gilmer, Joseph, 2011, Analysis of the deconstruction of Dyke Marsh, George Washington Memorial Parkway, Virginia—Progression, geologic and manmade causes, and effective restoration scenarios: U.S. Geological Survey Open-File Report 2010–1269, 80 p.

Executive Summary

Problem

Dyke Marsh, a freshwater wetland in northern Virginia and a migratory resource along the Atlantic Flyway, which is used by approximately 250 species of migratory birds, is eroding rapidly. The marsh was acquired in a congressional land trade agreement in 1959 and ceded to the National Park Service (NPS). At the time the NPS acquired it, dredge mining already had begun on its surface, and a preconditional 30-year mining agreement for direct dredging of the marsh had been stipulated. When mining ended in 1972 or 1973, the marsh had been transformed from an approximately 184-acre stable tidal wetland into a geologically unstable 83-acre remnant. Congress mandated its restoration in 1974. Unabated marsh loss has continued at this site since mining ceased, because the NPS was deeded a landform that inadvertently already had been destabilized geologically. When restoration was first mandated, the NPS had little knowledge of what the nature or scope of this problem was or how to fix it.

Background

The restoration of Dyke Marsh is important to the NPS not only because it is a migratory stop along the Atlantic Flyway but also because it also hosts state-listed (protected) plants and animals and is a frequently visited habitat resource for Bald Eagle and Peregrine Falcon in the Washington, D.C., metropolitan area. The NPS asked the U.S. Geological Survey (USGS) to study and report on all relevant aspects of this marsh loss problem. The USGS partnered with NPS personnel and several universities to address this issue.

The NPS had limited scientific knowledge about the physical aspects of Dyke Marsh prior to the present study. Its age and acreage were uncertain, with size estimates varying fourfold. Previous research at the marsh focused on other issues: marsh vegetation, bird nesting habitat, the general natural history of the marsh, invasive insects, a tidal creek study, and several feasibility studies for restoring the marsh. Prior to this study, no comprehensive analysis of the marsh's geologic history, destabilization, and degradation existed. The biological studies were important but were not of primary relevance for identifying the mechanism, rate, and scale of marsh erosion, geologic factors that are relevant to an effective restoration effort.

Focus of Study

The following questions are addressed in the report:

1. What is the most accurate age for the base of Dyke Marsh?

2. What was and is now the actual size of the main marsh (from 1937 to present)?

3. What were the pre- and post-mining configurations of Dyke Marsh (on the marsh and offshore)?

4. Is the marsh presently growing or shrinking? At what rate? What enabled it to grow?

5. What are the causes of the shoreline erosion? Is it continuous or episodic? How often does it occur?

6. What are the rates of shoreline erosion?

7. What geologic factors likely would diminish marsh erosion?

8. Is the marsh in a naturally sustainable state?

Findings

1. We secured an accurate, first-order age range for the marsh by ^{14}C radiometric dating of organic material at the marsh's base. Initial results indicate that the marsh started forming about 530 years ago (prior to Columbus' arrival). This corrected an earlier estimated age of 5,000 to 7,000 years before present.

2. We used historic aerial photographs and scaled them by laser-based range-finding equipment to establish accurate, gridded marsh acreages for a set of calendar years for which we had map or photographic documentation. The calculated acreages for those photographic years are ~184 (1937), ~169 (1959), ~83 (1976), ~79 (1987), ~69 (2002), and ~60 (2006).

3. Map and photographic evidence document that the marsh surface had a moderately stable configuration from 1864 to 1937 (for at least 73 years). This is the natural baseline the NPS is using for reference. Bathymetric charts from 1864 to 1931 indicate that the western river bottom abutting the marsh was shallow (2–4 feet deep), and had a moderately stable configuration as well (for at least 67 years).

The immediate post-mining marsh was ~83 acres, reduced from a high of 184 acres in 1937. The decrease in acreage was the result of mining, along with deconstruction, removal, or significant alteration of the tidal creeks that originally had been established naturally on the marsh. These tidal creeks are the primary source of sediment that is delivered to and sustains the marsh.

4. Photographic evidence shows that the post-mining marsh remnant is shrinking rapidly. Dyke Marsh has lost >25 percent of its remaining acreage to erosion between 1976 and 2006. Initial analyses of marsh cores indicate that the tidal creeks historically have deposited 3 to 5 millimeters of sediment onto the marsh surface annually (by tidal deposition), enough for the marsh to grow and sustain itself pre-mining.

5. Field evidence on the marsh shows that Potomac flooding from upriver was not the cause of marsh erosion. Rather, directional erosion indicators on the marsh suggest that storm waves driven northward up the Potomac River valley, from tropical storms and hurricanes in the summer and nor'easters in the winter, were the primary agents of marsh erosion. This erosion has progressed primarily from the southeast to the northwest. We calculated that the storm recurrence frequency at the marsh is every ~3 years on average, with 75 to 90 percent of the quiet (non-storm) intervals having an average of <1- to 3-year lulls between storm events. These estimates include only historic tropical storm and hurricane data analyzed from the National Oceanic and Atmospheric Administration for 1937 to 2009. Destructive storm events from the south were found to be common occurrences at this site.

6. Linear shoreline erosion at the marsh averages between 6 feet and 7.8 feet per year, measured in an east-to-west direction. This erosion is fragmenting the last significant tidal creek network on the marsh, reducing the ability of the marsh to deposit sediment and to rebuild itself. The erosion is decreasing the acreage of the marsh surface and thus decreasing marsh habitat for state-listed species, migratory waterfowl, and predatory birds (Bald Eagle and Peregrine Falcon).

7. Historically, the shallow western river bottom and a forested floodplain promontory south of the marsh (that extended ~1500 feet northeastward into the Potomac River) jointly buffered most storm activity directed toward the marsh. These enabled the marsh to keep a semistable configuration for at least 70 years. Dredge mining before 1959 removed those protections, destabilizing the marsh and exposing it to repeated storm erosion. Also, deep mining-scar channels (>25 feet below mean low water) now exist in the western river bottom adjacent to the present shoreline, cut into what originally was emergent marsh inside the park boundary. These mining channels have become active scour channels along this stretch of the Potomac, increasing the intensity of storm erosion at the shoreline, and adding to the marsh's instability.

8. We conclude that the marsh is not in a geologically sustainable state. The best present geologic evidence suggests Dyke Marsh will continue to be subjected to strong lateral shoreline erosion and stream piracy until (1) its former geological protections are restored by human intervention or (2) it is fully dismembered and eroded away by recurrent future storm activity (if left alone).

The storm recurrence estimate likely will increase in frequency once winter storms are analyzed and integrated into this dataset. However, erosion likely would diminish significantly and deposition would be enhanced if the marsh were protected from storm waves at its southern end (where the promontory previously existed), if the mining scar channels were rendered nonfunctional as scour channels, and if the outflow of the last major tidal creek were protected from further storm erosion and redirected back to its pre-mining orientation.

Contents

Figures

Tables

Analysis of the Deconstruction of Dyke Marsh, George Washington Memorial Parkway, Virginia: Progression, Geologic and Manmade Causes, and Effective Restoration Scenarios

By Ronald J. Litwin,[1] Joseph P. Smoot,[1] Milan J. Pavich,[1] Helaine W. Markewich,[2] Erik Oberg,[3] Ben Helwig,[3] Brent Steury,[3] Vincent L. Santucci,[3] Nancy J. Durika,[1] Nancy B. Rybicki,[4] Katharina M. Engelhardt,[5] Geoffrey Sanders,[3] Stacey Verardo,[6] Andrew J. Elmore,[5] and Joseph Gilmer[3]

Abstract

This report is a synthesis of the latest findings from an ongoing study of Dyke Marsh, an eroding freshwater tidal wetland that is scheduled for federal restoration. Its purpose is to provide an accurate and up-to-date temporal and geological framework for the marsh, of which most is new information (plus a compilation of historical and recent information), that is directly relevant to the restoration effort and also is relevant to short-term and long-term land management decisions regarding this natural resource.

Analysis of field evidence, aerial photography, and published maps has revealed an accelerating rate of erosion and marsh loss at Dyke Marsh, which now appears to put at risk the short term survivability of this marsh. The destabilization of Dyke Marsh is outlined here, spanning an approximately 70-year time interval (1940–2010). This freshwater tidal marsh has shifted from a semi-stable net depositional environment (1864–1937) into a strongly erosional one, during a time when it currently is in early-phase planning for comprehensive restoration. The marsh has been deconstructed over the past 70 years by a combination of manmade and natural causes. The marsh initially experienced a strong destabilizing period between 1940 and 1972 by direct dredge mining of the marsh surface. By 1976 the marsh had entered a net destructive phase, where it remains at present.

Photoanalysis of time-sequence aerial photographs of Dyke Marsh enabled us to calculate shoreline erosion estimates for this marsh over 19 years (1987–2006), as well as to quantify overall marsh acreage for 6 calendar years spanning an ~70 year interval (1937–2006). Photo overlay of a historic map enabled us to extend our whole-marsh acreage calculations back to 1883. Both sets of analyses were part of a geologic framework study in support of current efforts by the National Park Service (NPS) to restore this urban wetland. Two time intervals were selected for our shoreline erosion analyses, based on image quality and availability: 1987 to 2002, and 2002 to 2006.[7] The more recent time interval shows a marked increase in erosion in the southern part of Dyke Marsh, following a wave-induced breach of a small peninsula that had protected its southern shoreline. Field observations and analyses of annual aerial imagery between 1987 and 2006 revealed a progressive increase in wave-induced erosion that presently is deconstructing Hog Island Gut, the last significant tidal creek network within the Dyke Marsh. These photo analyses documented an overall average westward shoreline loss of 6.0 to 7.8 linear feet per year along the Potomac River during this 19-year time interval. Additionally, photographic evidence documented that lateral erosion now is capturing existing higher order tributaries in the Hog Island Gut. Wave-driven stream piracy is fragmenting the remaining marsh habitat, and therefore its connectivity, relatively rapidly, causing the effective mouth of the Hog Island Gut tidal network to retreat headward visibly over the past several decades. Based on our estimates of total marsh area in the Dyke Marsh derived from 1987 aerial imagery, as much as 12 percent of the central part of the marsh has eroded in the 19 year period we studied (or ~7.5 percent of the original ~78.8 acres of 1987 marshland). Shoreline loss estimates for marsh parcels north and south of our study area have not yet been analyzed, although annual aerial photos from 1987 to 2002 confirm visible progressive shoreline loss in those areas over this same time interval.

[1] U.S. Geological Survey, National Center, MS 926A, Reston, VA 20192.

[2] U.S. Geological Survey, 3039 Amwiler Rd., Suite 130, Peachtree Business Center, Atlanta, GA 30360.

[3] U.S. National Park Service, George Washington Memorial Parkway, Turkey Run Park, McLean, VA 22101.

[4] U.S. Geological Survey, National Center, MS 430, Reston, VA 20192.

[5] University of Maryland, Center for Environmental Studies, Appalachian Laboratory, Frostburg, MD 21532.

[6] AOES Department, George Mason University, MS5F2, Fairfax, VA 22030.

[7] More recently acquired imagery from 2005, 2007, and 2009 currently is being analyzed by several of the authors; those results will be presented elsewhere.

Purpose of Study

The U.S. Congress has mandated the restoration of Dyke Marsh (appendix 1), implicitly back to a naturally sustainable condition. A prerequisite to such an effective and sustainable restoration would be establishing an accurate geologic and temporal framework for the marsh, especially with respect to (1) estimating the marsh's pre-mining most stable configuration, (2) characterizing the nature and timing of subsequent changes to that semi-stable system, (3) characterizing the marsh's present condition, to determine the extent of the present marsh, to determine its aggradation rates, and to determine its present state of net loss or net gain, and (4) identifying those factors that promoted a geologically stable marsh in the past, as well as those factors necessary to reestablish a sustainable marsh. We address these factors in this report sequentially. Characterization of the marsh's present processes included field observations to determine the relative impact of ongoing constructive (aggradation) processes and destructive geologic processes on the marsh. It also included an analysis to determine the relative importance of episodic flooding of the adjacent Potomac River and wind-generated wave action against the present marsh's shoreline. Development of an accurate baseline for understanding the marsh's history, processes, and stressors will help to provide the NPS with the sound geological information needed to help them manage this freshwater wetland effectively.

Background

Dyke Marsh is the eroding remnant of a formerly extensive freshwater tidal marsh, adjacent to George Washington's Mount Vernon estate, and situated approximately 7 miles (mi) south of Washington, D.C., along the Potomac River's western shore (fig. 1). It is a migratory resource along the Atlantic Flyway and is used by approximately 250 species of migratory birds (Johnston, 2000). It is nesting habitat for several locally uncommon or state-listed (protected) species (Marsh Wren (*Cistothorus palustris*) and Least Bittern (*Ixobrychus exilis*)), and host to other state-listed species (Davis' Sedge (*Carex davisii*), appendix 2). It also is a frequent habitat resource for recently de-listed species or those uncommon to an urban setting, such as the Bald Eagle (*Haliaeetus leucocephalus*) the Peregrine Falcon (*Falco peregrinus*), and the River Otter (*Lutra canadensis*). As such, the importance of Dyke Marsh as a habitat resource for wildlife in the NPS system, especially in this urban setting, is well established.

Historically, the marsh appeared to be in a semistable configuration from at least 1883 to 1937, as documented by maps and a historic composite of aerial photos (fig. 2, appendix 3). When the George Washington Memorial Parkway (GWMP) acquired the marsh in 1959, it already showed visible evidence of destabilization (fig. 3). We attribute this largely to the direct and indirect effects of historic dredge

mining for sand and gravel, which occurred between ~1940 and 1972 (appendix 1). A significant portion of the original marsh acreage was removed during this operation. In the aftermath of this mining, the GWMP—which administers the Dyke Marsh—is working actively to restore the marsh to a naturally sustainable condition, as mandated by Congress (P.L. 86-41, P.L. 93-251, appendix 1). The GWMP is in the process of preparing an environmental impact statement as a necessary prerequisite for this restoration.

During 2009 and 2010 sitework at Dyke Marsh, several of the authors noted field evidence of strong erosion on the southern marsh and in the southern marsh woodland. This evidence prompted a time-series analysis of historic to recent aerial imagery of the marsh and documentation of these erosional features, resulting in this report.

Previous Studies

Previous studies at Dyke Marsh include a landmark tidal hydrology study (Myrick and Leopold, 1963) on a now mined-out tidal channel network that formerly occupied the northeastern quadrant of the 1960 marsh (tidal creek #2, this study, fig. 2). Since that time, studies involving Dyke Marsh have focused primarily on the vegetation community of the marsh and adjacent Potomac River bottom (Carter and others, 1985; Carter and Rybicki, 1986; Carter and others, 1994; Engelhardt, 2006; Hopfensperger and Engelhardt, 2007; Hopfensperger and Engelhardt, 2008), native and invasive insect species (Kjar and Barrows, 2004; Barrows and others, 2004, 2008; Barrows and Flint, 2009), avian nesting habitat (Spencer, 2000), denitrification processes (Hopfensperger and others, 2009), Dyke Marsh restoration feasibility studies (Palermo and Ziegler, 1976; Hopfensperger and others, 2007), an overview of Dyke Marsh's natural history (Johnston, 2000), and a bathymetry study (Normandeau Associates, 2009). No comprehensive analysis of the marsh's geologic history and degradation existed prior to this report.

Temporal Framework of Dyke Marsh: Revision of Age

This study updates the temporal framework of the marsh. We currently are in the process of establishing the age and progression of the marsh's initial development, by radiometric dating of core sediments at multiple sites across the marsh. This also will permit us to document and compare historic baseline accumulation rates for the marsh (spanning the past several centuries), for comparison to modern marsh accumulation data now being collected by several authors of this study. That portion of our study, addressing issues of current relative sea-level rise versus marsh accumulation, is in progress and its results will be reported elsewhere. The first results of our

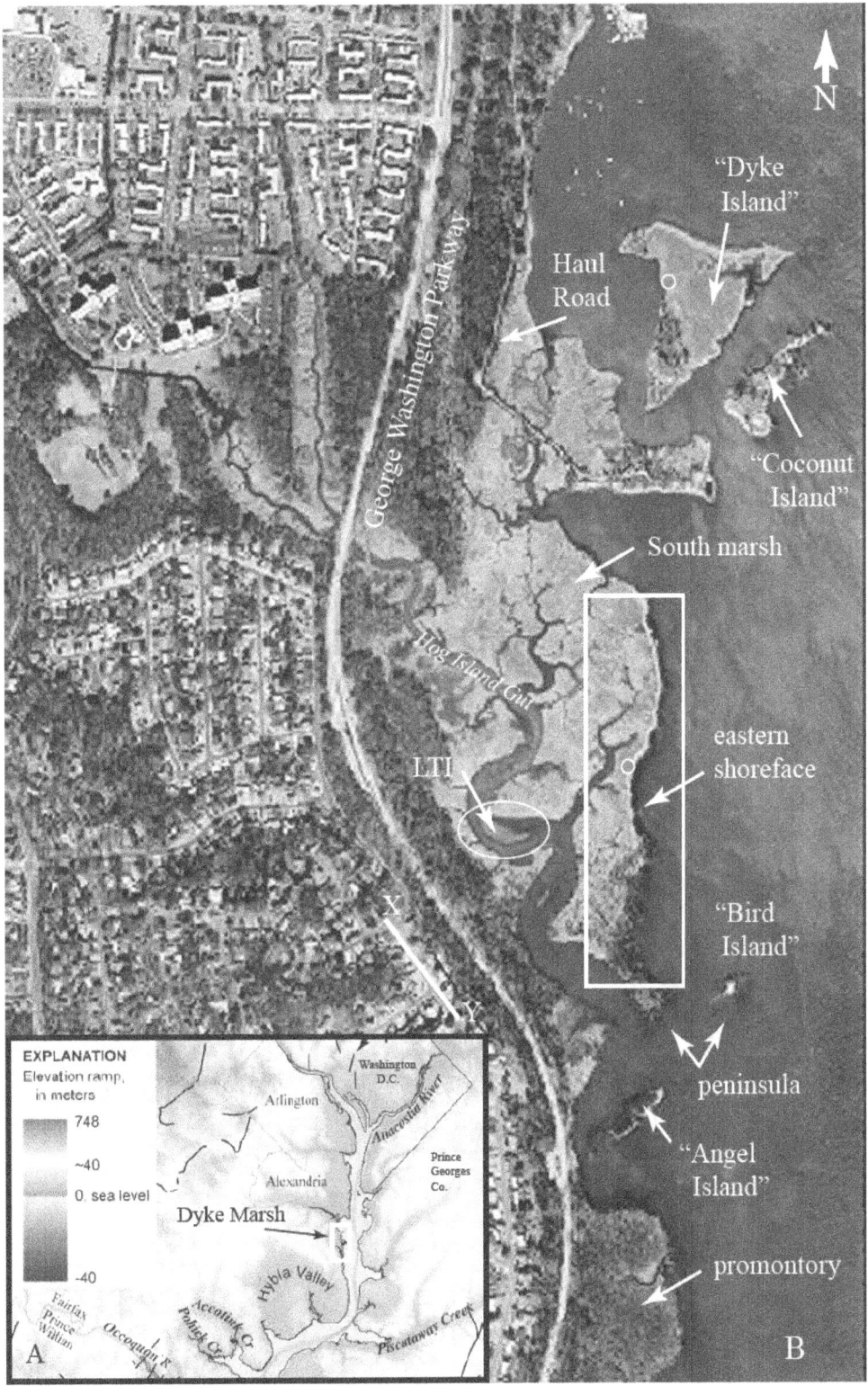

Figure 1. A, Site locality map of Dyke Marsh, south of Washington, D.C. (white box). B, A 2006 aerial image showing Accelerated Mass Spectrometry (AMS) ^{14}C sample locations (red dots) and field sites noted in this study. Island remnants of marsh are named here alphabetically (informal usage, south to north) as "Angel Island," "Bird Island," "Coconut Island," and "Dyke Island," for facilitating geographic reference in text. "LTI" (low tide indicator) marks the persistent landform in Hog Island Gut that was used to confirm low tide conditions (~0–1.5 ft above mean low water) in the photo series we analyzed for this report.

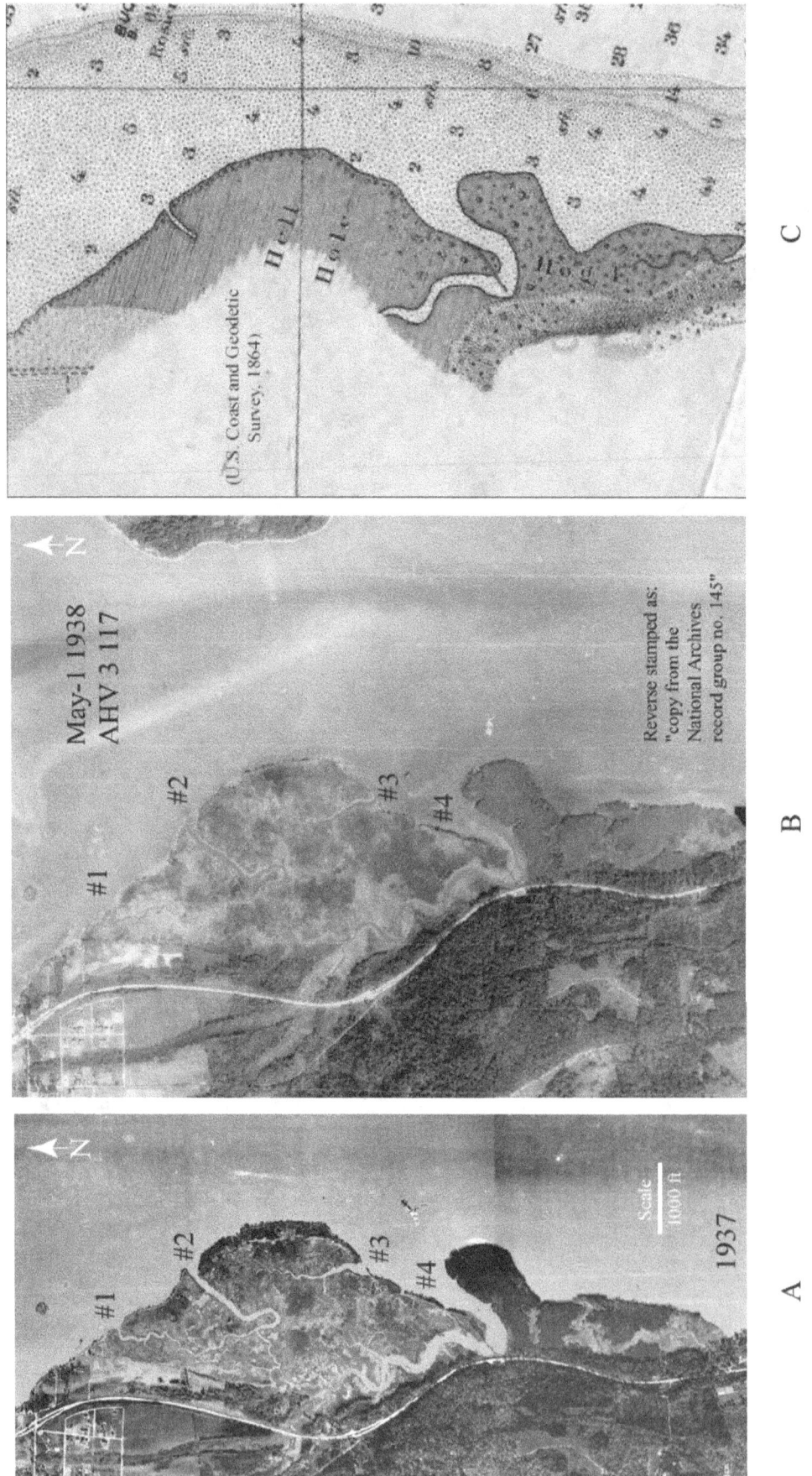

Figure 2.   Stable marsh shore profile. A, A 1937 aerial image of Dyke Marsh. B, A 1938 aerial image of Dyke Marsh. Tidal creeks on the marsh are numbered north to south. C, An 1864 map of Dyke Marsh.

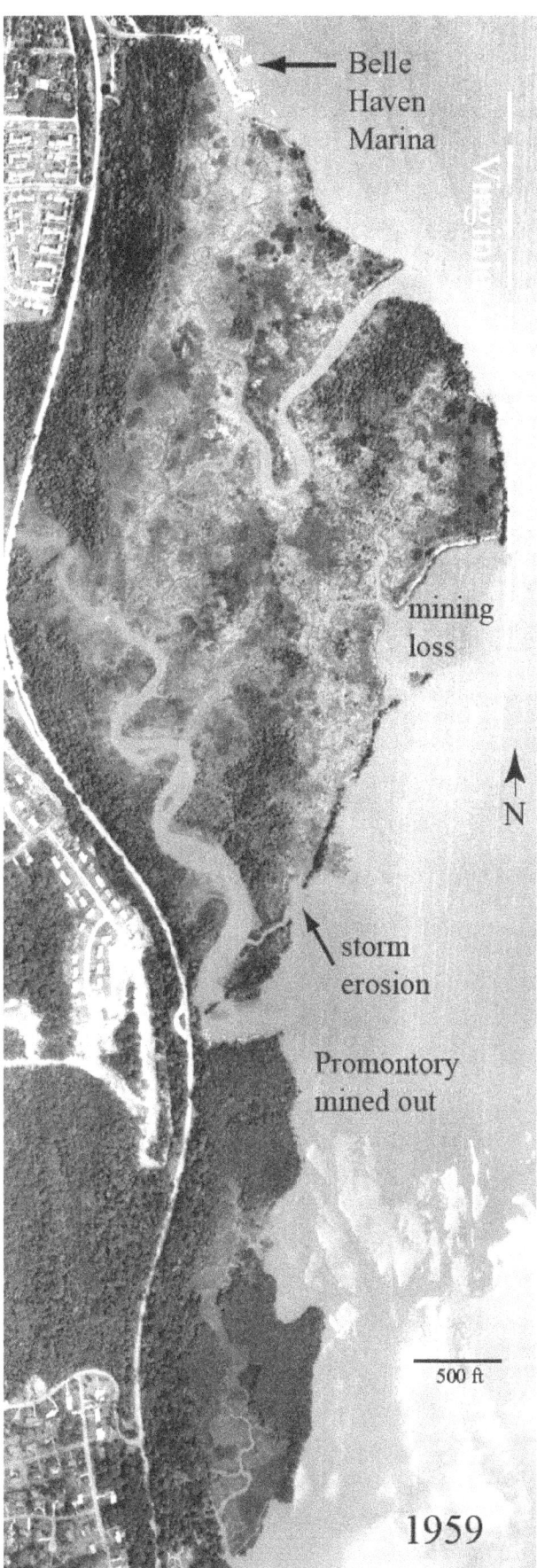

Belle
Haven
Marina

mining
loss

↑
N

storm
erosion

Promontory
mined out

500 ft

1959

Accelerator Mass Spectrometry (AMS) carbon-14 (^{14}C) analyses suggest that Dyke Marsh is approximately 530 ± 70 cal yr B.P. (~1480 A.D., this study, based on calibration per CALIB 5.0.1; Stuiver and Reimer, 1993; Reimer and others, 2004) near its organic-rich base in the north, and approximately 360 ± 70 cal yr B.P. in the south (~1650 A.D., table 1, 2-sigma errors). Fossil pollen evidence, in conjunction with these radiocarbon age estimates, suggests the marsh formed as a naturally derived, pre-Colonial feature that was fully established by the Late Middle Ages (~1400 A.D.). Our radiometric age analyses supersede the older empirical estimate of the marsh's age (5,000–7,000 B.P., in Myrick and Leopold, 1963) and further suggest that the marsh's initial development was not primarily the result of deforestation and consequent sediment runoff (siltation) into Hunting Creek during European Colonial agricultural expansion.

The unconsolidated sediments underlying the organic marsh are still of indeterminate age and are a focus of our current research. Dated shallow subsurface sediments from nearby sites, adjacent to the Potomac but south of Dyke Marsh, are of Late Pleistocene age (~17,000–50,000 B.P.; Markewich and others, 2009; Pavich and others, 2010). Shallow surface cores that extend below mean sea level (the approximate mean water level of the tidal Potomac), but are sited west of Dyke Marsh, also are of Late Pleistocene age (~24,000–130,000 B.P.; +15 meters above sea level (m asl) to −20 m asl; Litwin and others, 2010). However, those generally occur at a higher base elevation than the sediments underpinning the marsh at Dyke Marsh and thus may represent older terrace deposits lateral to the Potomac. Dyke Marsh basal sediments may be as young as Holocene in age (≤10,000 B.P.).

Table 1.   Initial radiocarbon ages and calibration[1] for Dyke Marsh cores DM1 and DM2.

[cm, centimeters; mm/yr, millimeters per year]

Sample	Core depth (cm)	^{14}C radiocarbon age	2-sigma error	Calibrated age	Accumulation rate (mm/yr)
DM1-60 (reworked)	60	300	90	1560 A.D.	1.34
DM1-162	162	395	70	1480 A.D.	3.06
DM2-143	143	230	70	1660 A.D.	4.09
DM2-143	143	230	70	1770 A.D.[2]	5.98
DM2-189	189	255	70	1649 A.D.	5.25

[1] Per Calib 5.0.1; Stuiver and Reimer (1993), Reimer and others (2004).

[2] More probable age.

Figure 3.   A 1959 aerial photo of Dyke Marsh, the year of acquisition by the NPS. Note that the marsh was altered from its natural state by construction of a marina, initial shoreface mining, storm erosion, and the removal by dredging of the forested sandy promontory south of the main marsh.

Geological Framework of Marsh

Estimation of Acreage of Marsh

Existing estimates of the main marsh's acreage vary. Johnston (2000) implied that the marshland component within the parcel known as Dyke Marsh comprised ~140 acres (35 percent of an estimated ~400-acre mixed-vegetation total acreage). The NPS website for Dyke Marsh includes the marsh only as part of a larger "485 acres of tidal marsh, flood plain, and swamp forest" (http://www.nps.gov/gwmp/dyke-marsh.htm). As a prerequisite to measuring shoreline loss rates on the marsh, we needed to establish accurate acreage estimates for the whole marsh over our study interval (1937–2006).

For this purpose we used photoanalysis to calculate Dyke Marsh's actual marsh acreage component at seven points in time: 1883, 1937, 1959, 1976, 1987, 2002, and 2006. All photos were verified to represent low tide conditions (~0–1.5 ft above mean low water). We confirmed this by the emergence of a persistent landform in Hog Island Gut (fig. 1, "LTI", or low tide indicator) that is fully emergent at low tide and fully

inundated at high tide. Additionally we confirmed low tide conditions in the photos by inundation of the marsh at its distal tributaries. The map-based 1883 estimate was verified as accurate in its survey by registration onto our 1937 aerial photograph. We calculated acreage by tiling 2,500-square-foot (ft^2) grid cells (50 ft × 50 ft; scaled to the photograph) across the marsh portion of the 1987 aerial photo. Smaller polygons were created by halving our standard grid cell horizontally, vertically, and diagonally; each of those polygons respectively bounded a 1,250-ft^2 area. All other photos and map images were superimposed and registered by multiple fixed reference points to this base photograph. The 50 ft scaled grid cell was calculated directly from a field-based laser transect we measured within the residential area visible to the southwest of the marsh (fig. 1). We did not include smaller marsh occurrences south of the truncated promontory (on the northern end of Hog Island) or west of the George Washington Parkway in our acreage estimate. The results of our analyses are presented in figure 4 and table 2.

Our post-1972 (post-mining) acreage calculations are considerably less than any other present estimates for the marsh of which we are aware. Our current best calculation

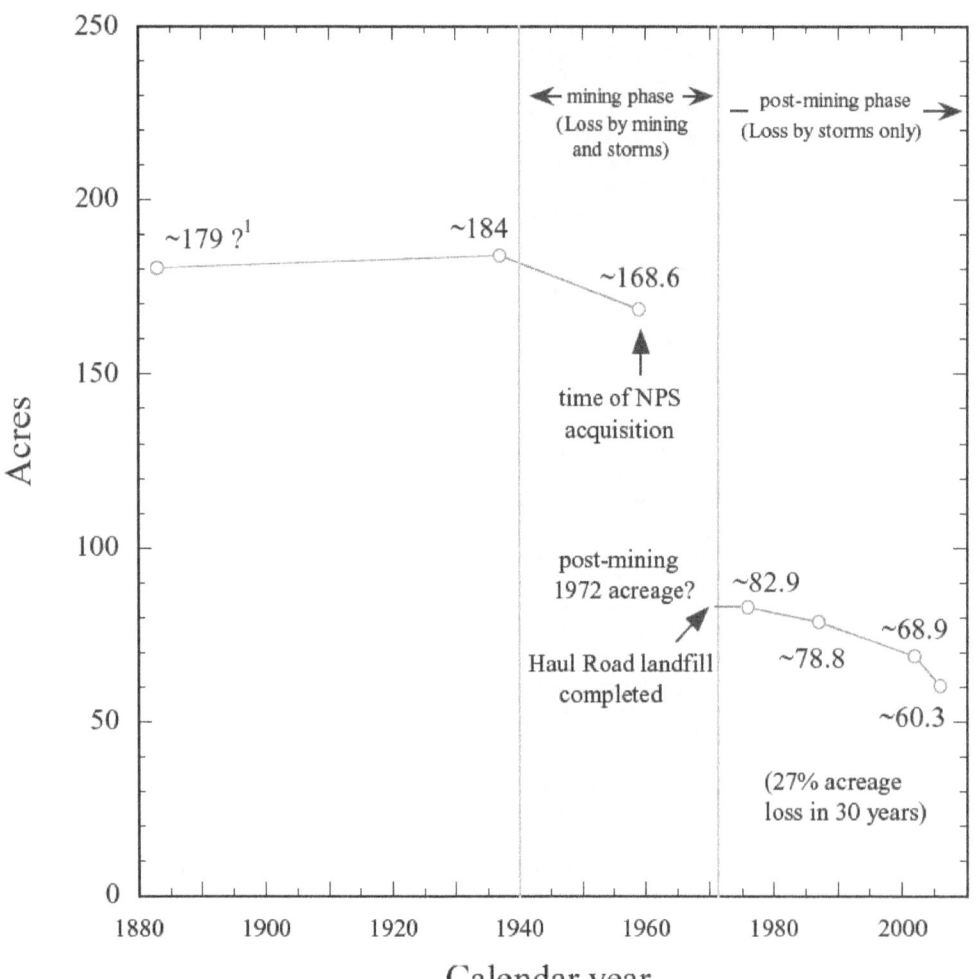

Figure 4. Photoanalysis of the deconstruction of Dyke Marsh wetland (excluding Hog Island). Calculated marsh acreages over the past ~120 years, excluding Hog Island and distal marsh east of George Washington Parkway.

[1] Estimate based on image overlay of 1883 map and 1937 photo (using fig. 2A and fig. 5A).

Table 2. Initial photo-based acreage estimates for Dyke Marsh (1883–2006).

Photo year	Acres (North Parcel)	Acres (Central Parcel)	Acres (South Parcel)	Total acres	Figure
1883				178.89	8F
1937	95.94	81.94	6.20	184.08	6B
1959	92.42	71.55	4.68	168.65	6D
1976	34.05	44.49	4.45	82.99	7B
1987	31.45	43.33	3.99	78.77	7D
2002	28.31	37.63	3.01	68.95	8B
2006	25.30	32.76	2.21	60.27	8D

for the size of the main marsh after cessation of dredging is ~83 acres (table 2). Our evidence further suggests that the current size (2010) of the entire main marsh is less than 60 acres, as bounded on the north by the access road to Belle Haven Marina, on the south by Hog Island, and on the west by the George Washington Parkway.

Estimating the Historic Stable Configuration for Dyke Marsh

Historical documents helped us to identify the most recent semi-stable configuration of Dyke Marsh. The largest areal configuration of the marsh that we calculated was for the ~54 year interval between 1883 and 1937. The maximum size of the main marsh that we calculated was about 180–184 acres, exclusive of major tidal creeks. This estimate is ~28 percent larger than Johnston's (2000) estimate. Two photos provide evidence of its maximum extent. The 1937 aerial photo composite (fig. 2A) and the aerial photo of May 1, 1938 (fig. 2B; single frame), both show the largest known expression of the marsh. They were taken just before the onset of dredge mining at the site. The same shoreline configuration seen in the 1937 and 1938 photos also is present in an 1864 map of the marsh (fig. 2C), indicating a minimum 74-year period of semi-stable marsh shoreline. These three documents collectively provided us a baseline for the most stable configuration of the marsh proper. The offshore data that documented the analogous stable river-bottom baseline configuration of the Potomac, for that area east of and adjacent to the marsh, are found in bathymetry charts from 1864, 1883, 1906, and 1931 (fig. 2C; fig. 5; appendix 3). They document a minimum semi-stable baseline of 67 years.

Characterizing the Nature and Timing of Changes to the Marsh (1937–2010)

Reduction of Original Acreage by Mining

Dredge mining consumed much of the original marsh acreage directly, from ~1940 to 1972. The Smoot Sand and Gravel Comp. maintained an active mining lease on the marsh at the time the land transferred to GWMP oversight in 1959, as part of the land acquisition agreement (appendix 1A). The complete acreage lost directly to mining is unknown. However, we were able to calculate a dependable estimate of mining loss (excluding Hog Island) by comparing available aerial imagery from 1937, 1959, 1976, and 1987 (figs. 6–8; table 2). The 1937 acreage estimated above (fig. 6A, table 2) was ~184 acres, and documents the marsh in its immediately pre-mined state. The 1959 acreage (fig. 6C) is ~169 acres, suggesting that dredge mining had consumed approximately 15 acres north of Hog Island by the time the NPS inherited this land parcel; the conspicuous promontory at the north end of Hog Island had been mined out previously, and almost entirely, soon after dredge operations first commenced. The 1976 and 1987 acreage calculated here (fig. 7) are ~83 and ~79 acres, suggesting that ~86 acres were dredged from the marsh between the time the land was acquired by the NPS and mining operations ceased. This estimate for mined acreage from the main part of the marsh is consistent with the stated agreement in Public Law 86-41, section 3 (appendix 1, 85 acres). We therefore estimate the maximum total marsh acreage lost to mining to be ~101 acres, exclusive of mining on Hog Island. This represents 54 percent of the entire 1937 marsh, or an area ~167 percent as large as the total 2006 main marsh remnant.

We cannot determine conclusively what part of this 101 acres may have been lost to storm erosion during the years that the marsh was under active mining. However, evidence presented in table 2 suggests that the loss attributed to storm erosion immediately after mining ended (1976–1987) was ~4 acres in 11 years, yielding a storm erosion rate of ~0.364 acres per year. That erosion rate (0.364 acres/yr) multiplied by the total years of mining (32) yields a tentative estimate of ~11.6 total acres for potential storm erosion during the active mining years. This is perhaps as much as ~11 percent of the acreage lost between 1940 and 1972, and is possible because the promontory had been mined out and storm waves could more easily reach the marsh. This suggests that somewhere between ~90 and ~101 acres of marshland were lost in total to mining, on the main part of the marsh.

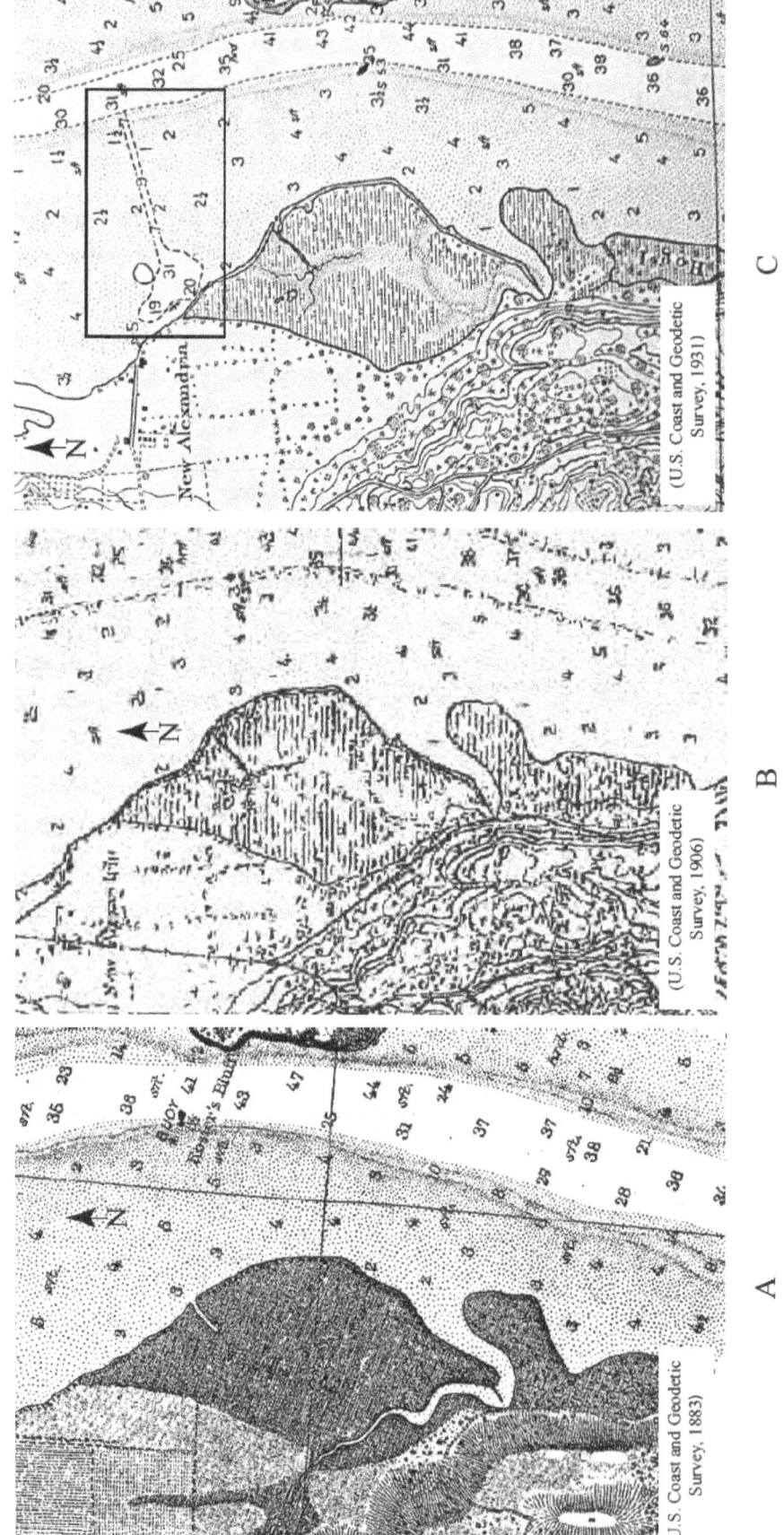

Figure 5.   Baseline river-bottom configuration. A, An 1883 bathymetric map of marsh area (excerpt). B, A 1906 bathymetric map of marsh area (excerpt). C, A 1931 bathymetric map of marsh area (excerpt), showing initial river-bottom dredging toward Dyke Marsh, for river traffic at the port of [New] Alexandria, Va.

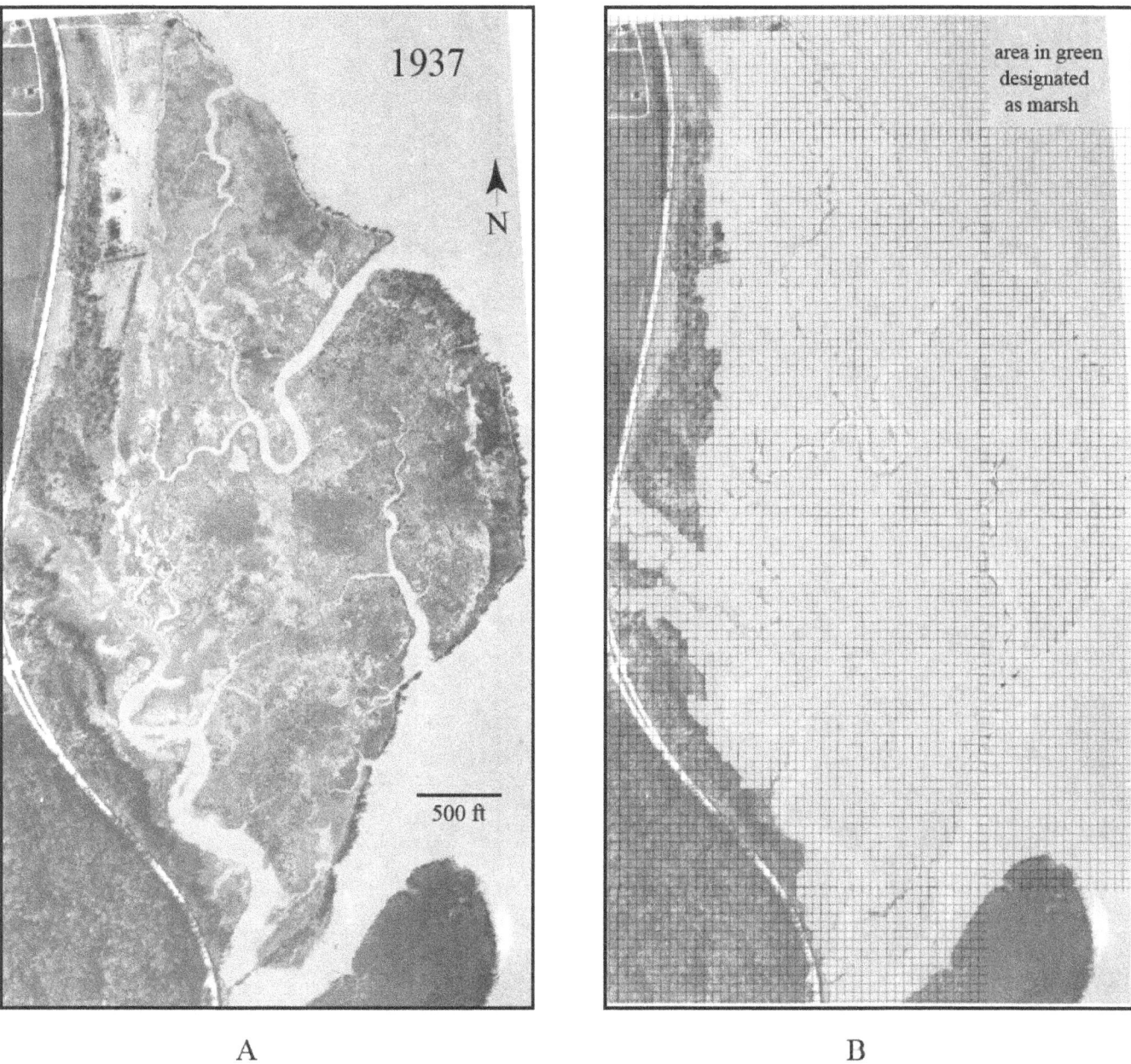

1937

N

500 ft

area in green
designated
as marsh

A

B

Figures 6A and 6B. Aerial photos and gridded estimates of acreage (table 2) for 1937. Grid cells are scaled to 50 ft x 50 ft, on the basis of a laser-based ground calibration line (165 m ± 1m length; see fig. 12C). Pink grid cells denote meadow acreage that converted to forest by 1959.

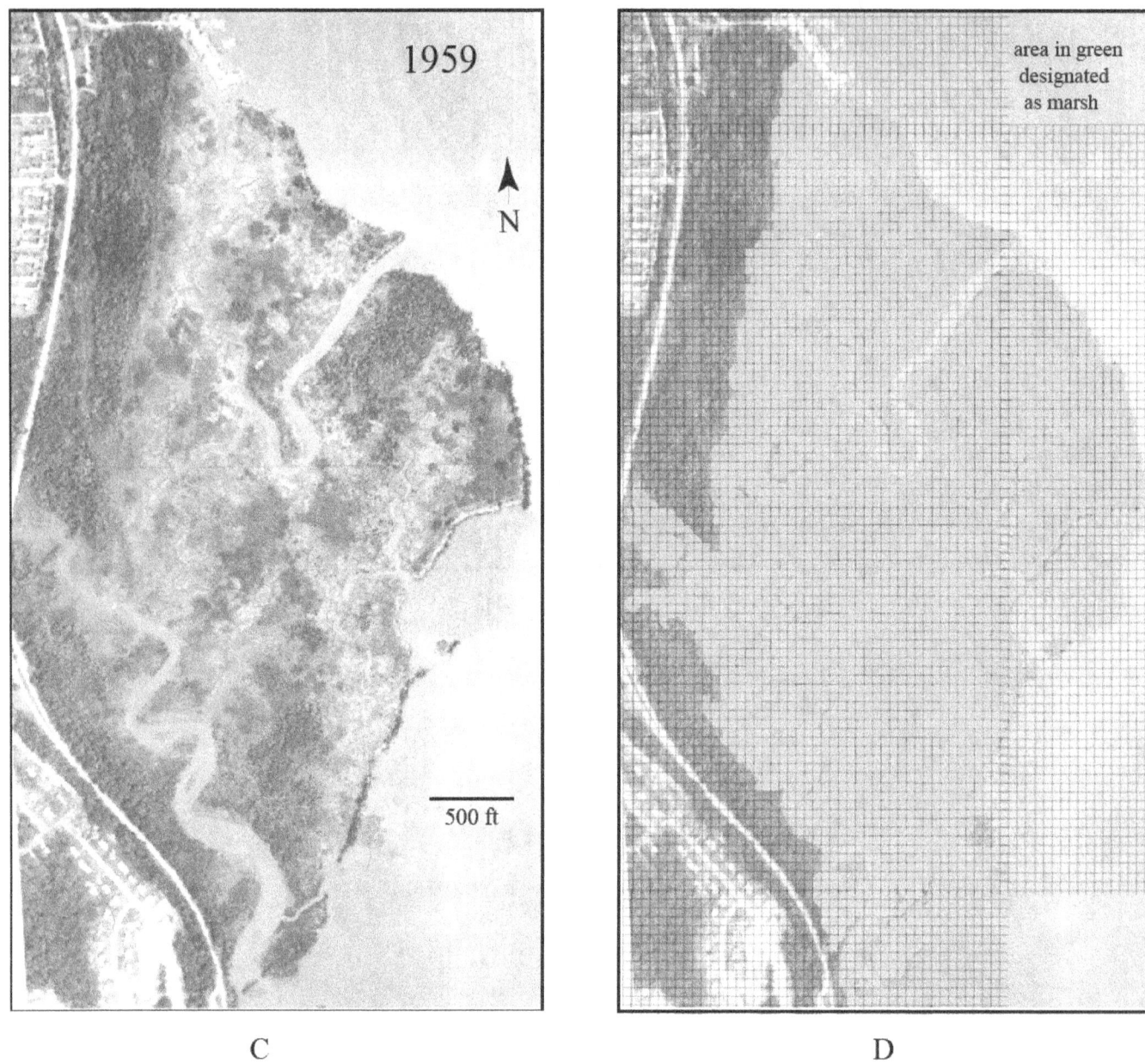

Figures 6C and 6D.   Aerial photos and gridded estimates of acreage (table 2) for 1959. Grid cells are scaled to 50 ft x 50 ft, on the basis of a laser-based ground calibration line (165 m ± 1m length; see fig. 12C).

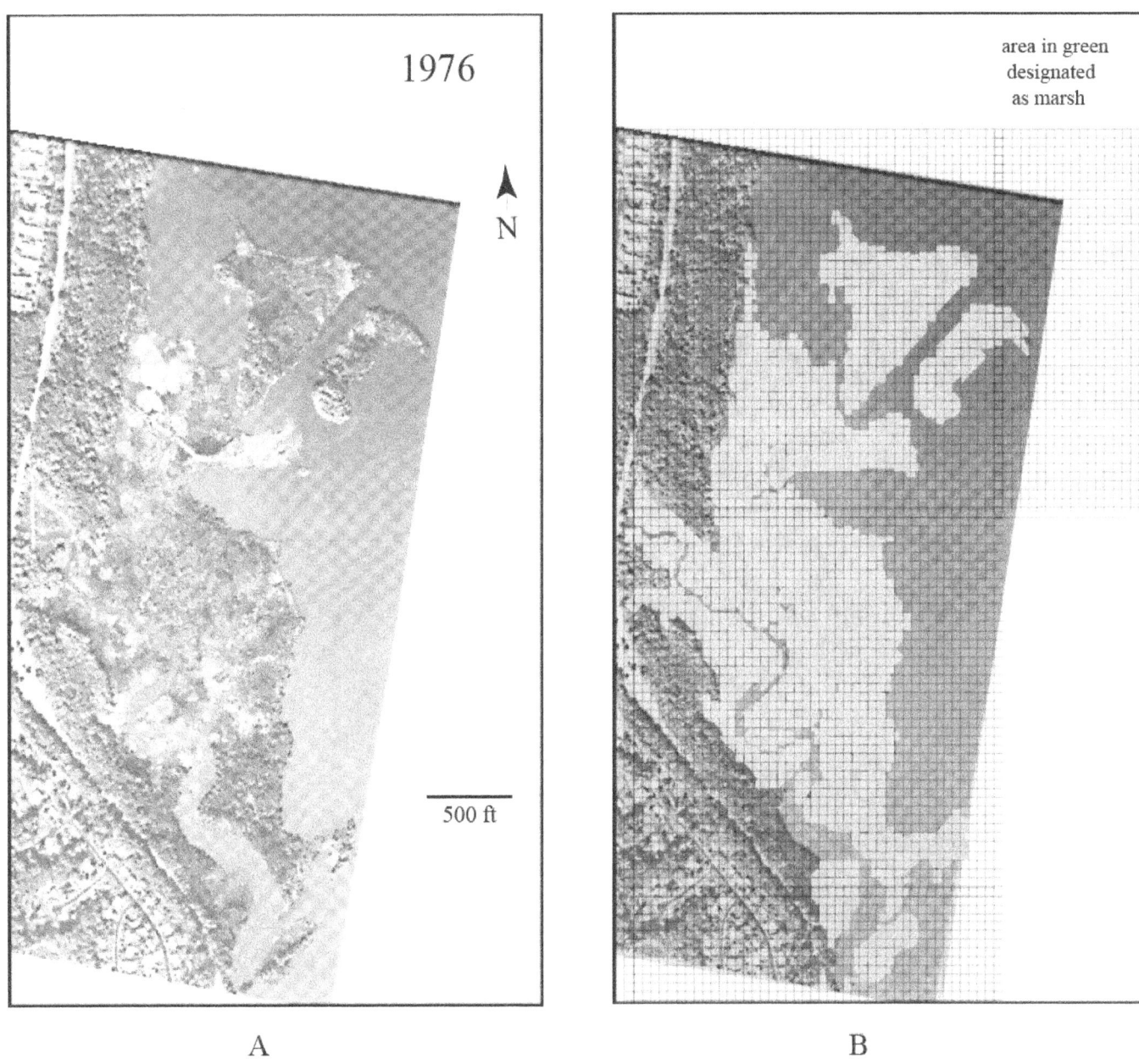

Figures 7A and 7B. Aerial photos and gridded estimates of acreage (table 2) for 1976. Grid cells are scaled to 50 ft x 50 ft, on the basis of a laser-based ground calibration line (165 m ± 1m length; see fig. 12C).

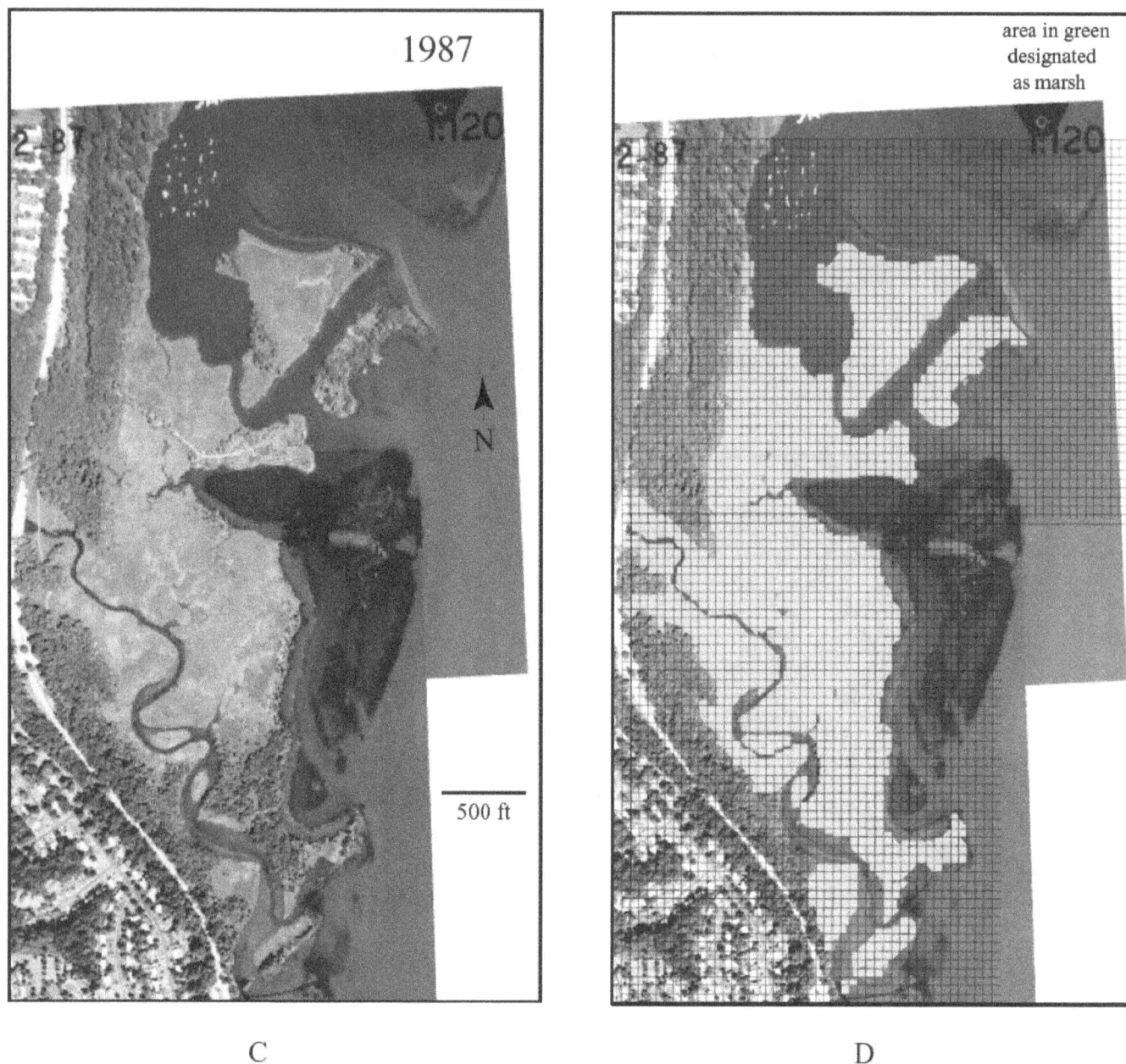

C

D

Figures 7C and 7D.   Aerial photos and gridded estimates of acreage (table 2) for 1987. Grid cells are scaled to 50 ft x 50 ft, on the basis of a laser-based ground calibration line (165 m ± 1m length; see fig. 12C).

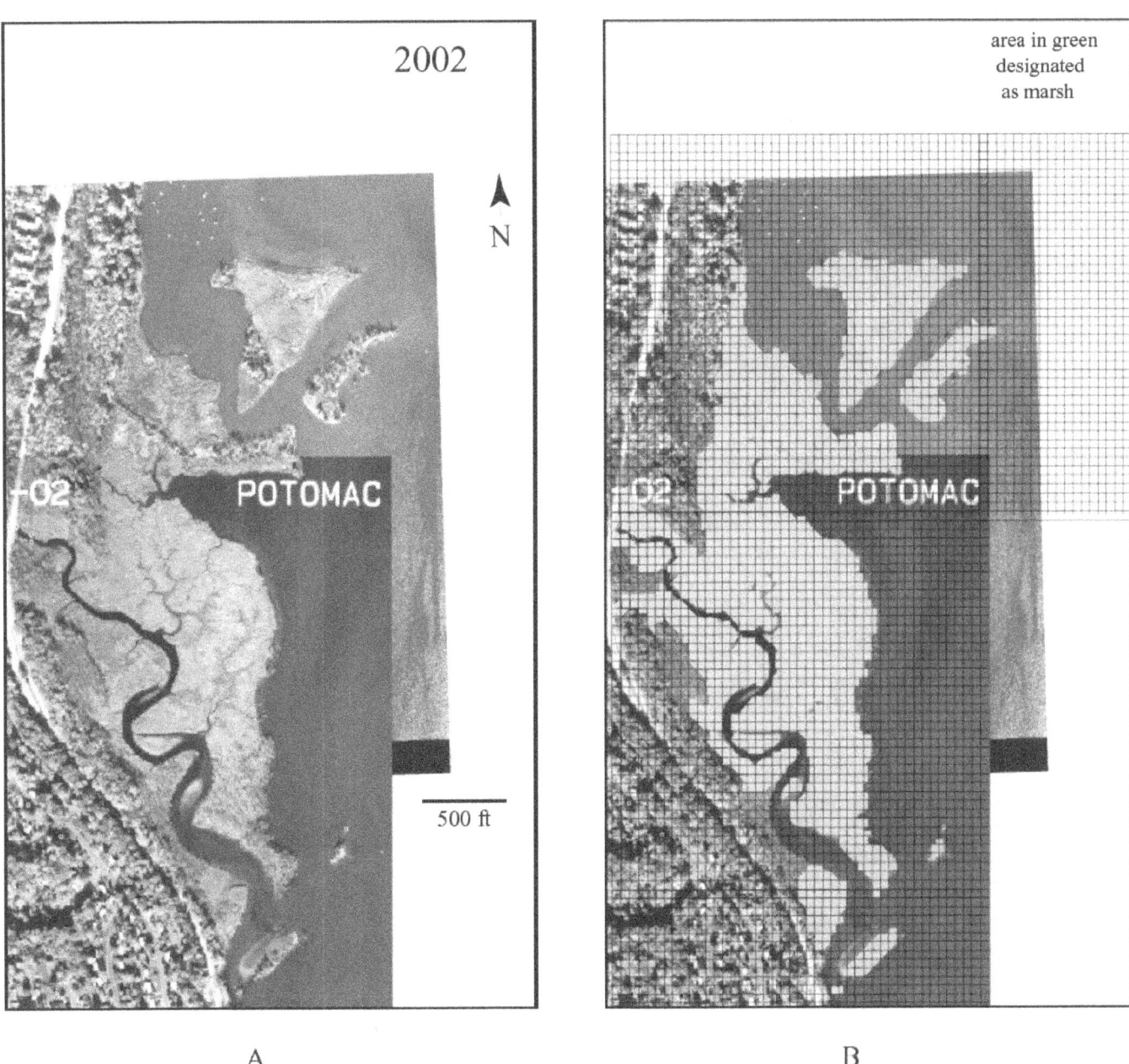

Figures 8A and 8B.   Aerial photos and gridded estimates of acreage (table 2) for 2002.

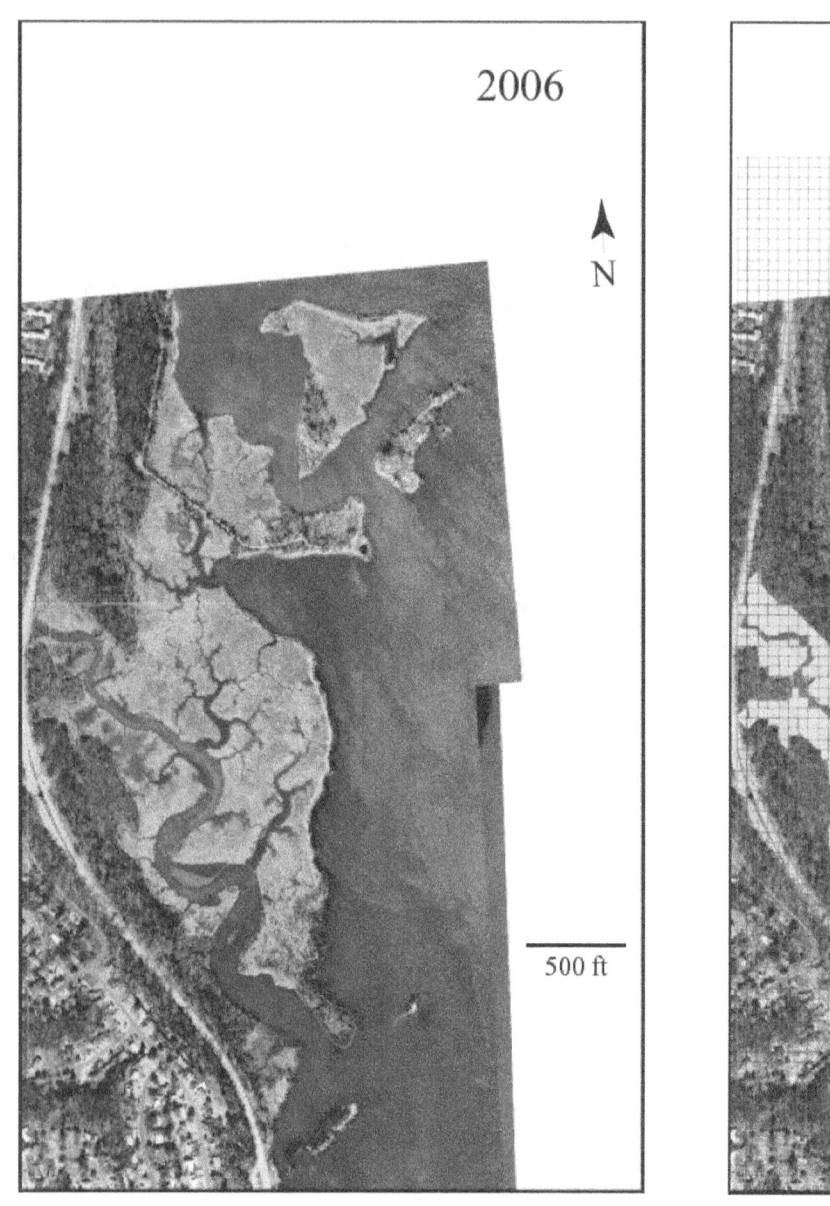

2006

N

500 ft

C

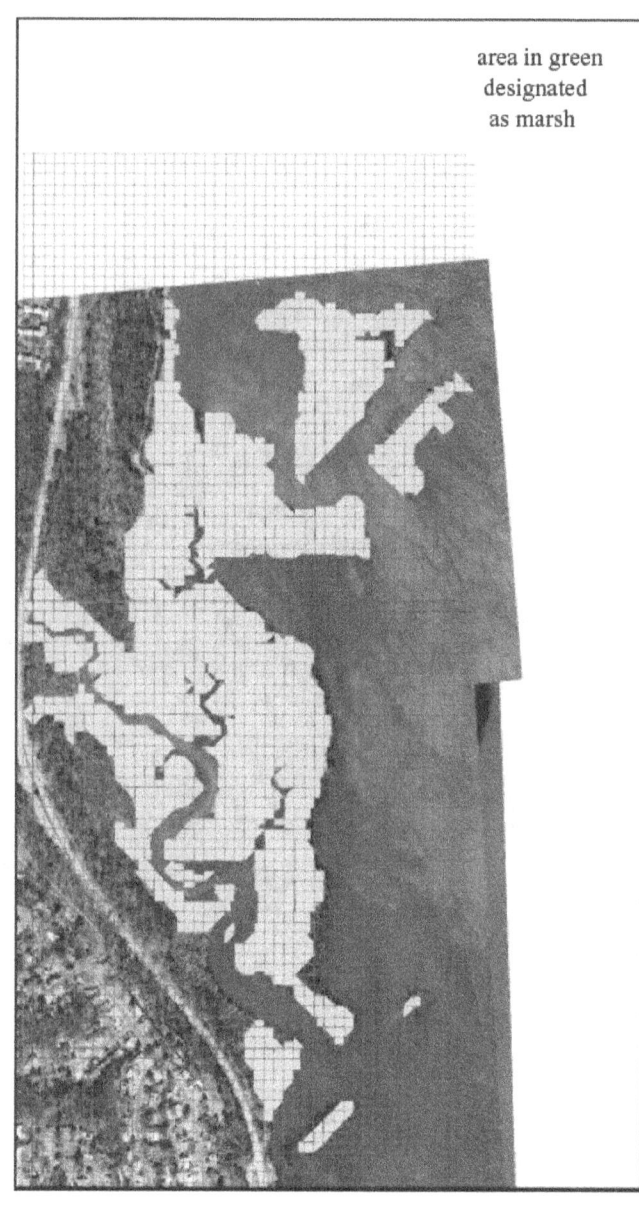

area in green
designated
as marsh

D

Figures 8C and 8D.   Aerial photos and gridded estimates of acreage (table 2) for 2006.

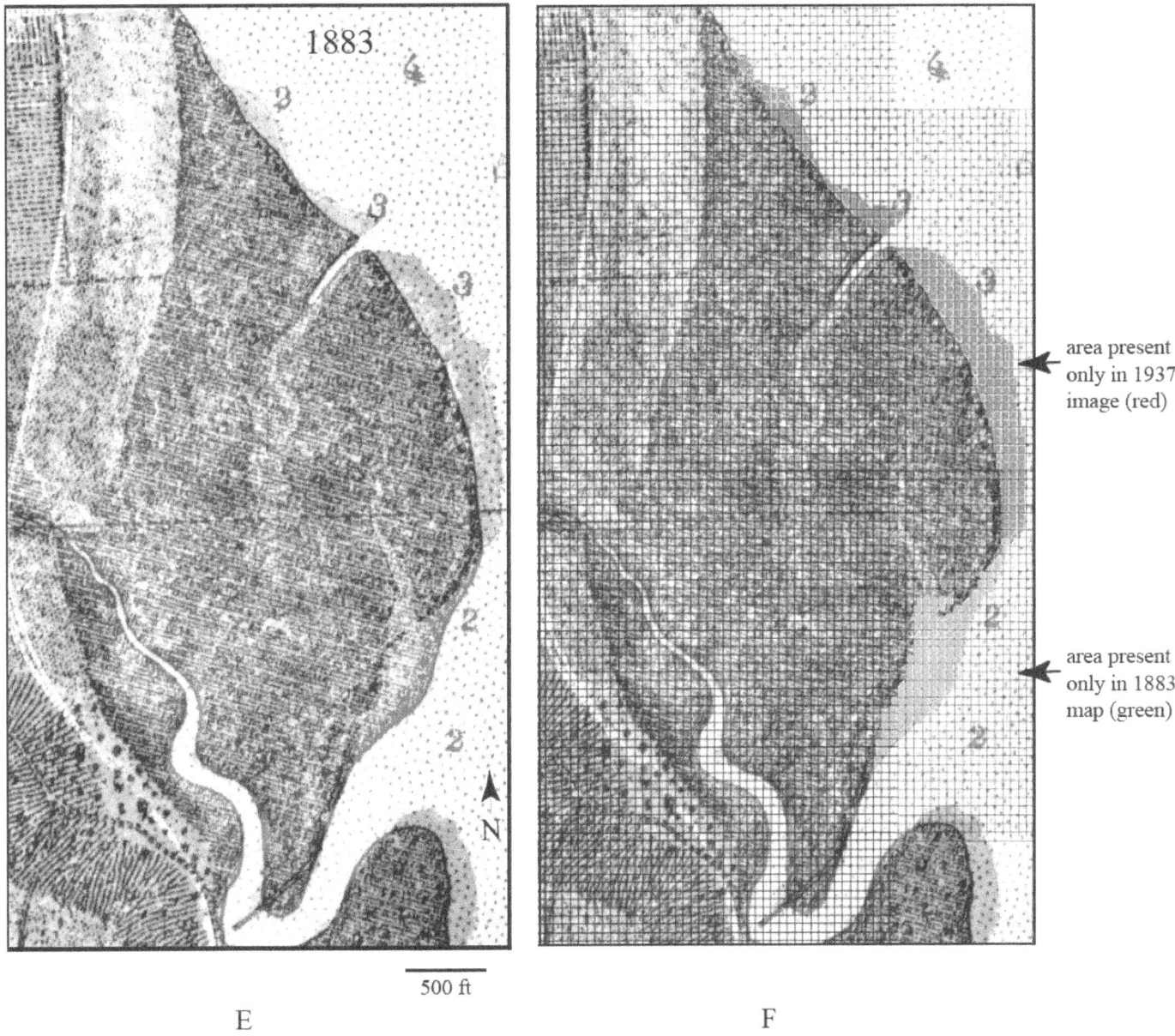

500 ft

E   F

Figures 8E and 8F.   Gridded estimate of 1883 map (E,F) was accomplished by map overlay onto the oldest known aerial photograph (E; 1937; see fig. 2C and fig. 9A for original map and photo). Overlay of the 1883 map and the 1937 photo (E) suggests that the northeastern ~150–200' perimeter strip of land on the 1937 image probably is landfill that had been artificially dumped to expand the marsh (post-1883), with a new dyke road built on that expansion (fig. 8F, red polygons). By contrast, the shoreline just north of the mouth of Hog Island Gut was mapped as larger in acreage in 1883 than the 1937 photo indicates (fig. 8F, green polygons). Given the registration match between many of the physiographic features on the map and image, we consider the 1883 map to be reasonably accurate. The 1883 acreage was derived by adding the green polygons and subtracting the red polygons from our 1937 photo-based acreage. Although this map appears to be accurate, we are less confident of this (map based) estimate than we are of our photo-based estimates.

Deconstruction of Tidal Creek Networks by Mining

Dredging did not just remove terrestrial acreage from Dyke Marsh. It also dismantled the tidal creek feeder system that sustained sedimentation across the marsh. In the 1937–1938 marsh baseline configuration, four primary tidal creek networks were established on the marsh (fig. 2). Three of these had terminal outflows that trended to the northeast, against the north-to-south streamflow of the Potomac River. This outflow orientation likely had an asymmetric effect on the timing of the filling and draining phases of the tidal creeks on the marsh during each tidal cycle, which ultimately favored growth of the marsh (accretion). This idea is consistent with evidence in Myrick and Leopold (1963, their figs. 9 and 10), who charted the tidal cycle in one of them (fig. 2 this study, creek #2). Their analysis of "Wrecked Recorder Creek" demonstrated that it did have an asymmetric timing to its tidal cycling.[8]

One effect of having a northeasterly terminal outflow (having drainages oriented counter to the Potomac River flow) was that it probably enhanced asymmetry in the timing of the filling and draining phases of these tidal creeks. Sediment-laden water likely was held in the marsh longer during the ebb-tide phase (draining phase), because the draining of the tidal creeks was impeded by the combined effects of oppositional flow from the Potomac and the relatively delayed ebbing tide in this stretch of the Potomac. Therefore, ebb tide on the marsh itself reached its local maximum velocity late in the waning cycle, when the ebbing tide on the Potomac River had dropped sufficiently to enable the tidal creeks also to drain. This is important because it effectively prolonged inundation of the marsh surface during each tidal cycle, and suspended sediments therefore had more time to settle out and to be trapped by marsh vegetation (Stevenson and others, 1988; Madsen and others, 2001; Pasternak and Brush, 2002; Nyman and others, 2006). This likely enhanced marsh growth and helped to build and maintain the stable 1937 configuration. Note that creek #3 probably also was impeded during its ebb phase but probably by a larger neighboring tidal creek (creek #4, Hog Island Gut, or HIG) rather than by the Potomac River itself.

This diurnal sediment delivery network to the marsh was disrupted as mining strongly reconfigured the terminal outflows of creeks #3 and #4 by 1959 (fig. 9A, B). The outflow of tidal creek #1 was altered by 1959 as a result of construction of a marina at the north end of the marsh. By 2006, tidal creek networks #1, #2, and #3 had been totally deconstructed by mining (fig. 9C). Only tidal creek #4 (HIG) remained. By 2006, this solitary surviving tidal creek network of the original 1937 marsh (HIG) also was being deconstructed, but by geologic forces activated by alteration of its original profile during mining.

Changing the Stabilizing Geomorphic Features On and Adjacent to the 1937 Marsh

The third effect that mining had at Dyke Marsh was to alter the geologic setting of the marsh, which initially had contributed to the marsh's development and to its protection in that location. Mining activity specifically altered two separate protective features for the marsh. The first of these was the low-elevation forested promontory at the south end of the marsh, on Hog Island. Originally this promontory formed the southern shoreline of HIG. It was mined out shortly after 1937 and prior to 1959 (figs. 2, 3, 9). The promontory performed several geologically important functions at this site. It comprised the southernmost shoreline of HIG, thereby directing its outflow northeastward. It also was a barrier that was low enough to be fully breached when the Potomac flooded, thus minimizing funneling of floodwater up the HIG. Also, it protected the southern end of the marsh from wind-driven storm waves from the south (see "Characterizing Present Processes Operating on the Marsh").

The second protective feature of the marsh that was altered by mining was located adjacent to the marsh, that is, the topography and bathymetry of the western edge of the Potomac River itself. Documents from 1883, 1906, and 1931 (fig. 5; appendix 3) show that the original stable river bottom formed a shallow slope grading from a western shoreline at the Virginia/Maryland border to a singular deep channel on the Maryland (eastern) side. The western shoreline of the river and the western river-bottom configuration were changed considerably by 1992 (see below).

The GWMP contracted to have several bathymetric surveys done in 1992 and 2009 of the waterway inside the Dyke Marsh boundary (where marsh had existed previously; fig. 10). These surveys documented a deep bifurcating channel incised into an irregular but shallow river bottom; it is oriented subparallel to shoreline. The deep bifurcated channel is present as a well-established feature inside the Dyke Marsh boundary in both surveys and is established where terrestrial marsh existed in 1959 (compare figs. 3, 5, and 10). The deep channel most likely represents either the remnant of a barge shipping lane created for and during the dredge operation, or simply the deepest extent of sand and gravel retrieval, as it is notably deeper than the original baseline river bottom (fig. 5). Historical documents suggest that the mining agreement permitted dredging of sediment down to 30 ft below low water [of the Potomac waterline] (appendix 1D). This maximum mining depth limit is only several feet deeper than the relict river bottom scars documented in the 2009 bathymetry report (Normandeau Associates, 2009, cross section B-B′), suggesting that the deep channeling on what was formerly marsh surface likely is a direct artifact of that mining. This offshore channel increased visibly in width and depth between 1992 and 2009, decades after mining had ceased on the marsh, probably as repeated discharges of Potomac floodwater converted it into a secondary erosional river channel.

---

[8] The probable position for this wrecked tidal gauge (metal framework) was relocated in April 2010 by three of the authors during fieldwork for this study. Its geographic coordinates are 38 46′ 11.9″ N., 77 02′ 53.2″ W.

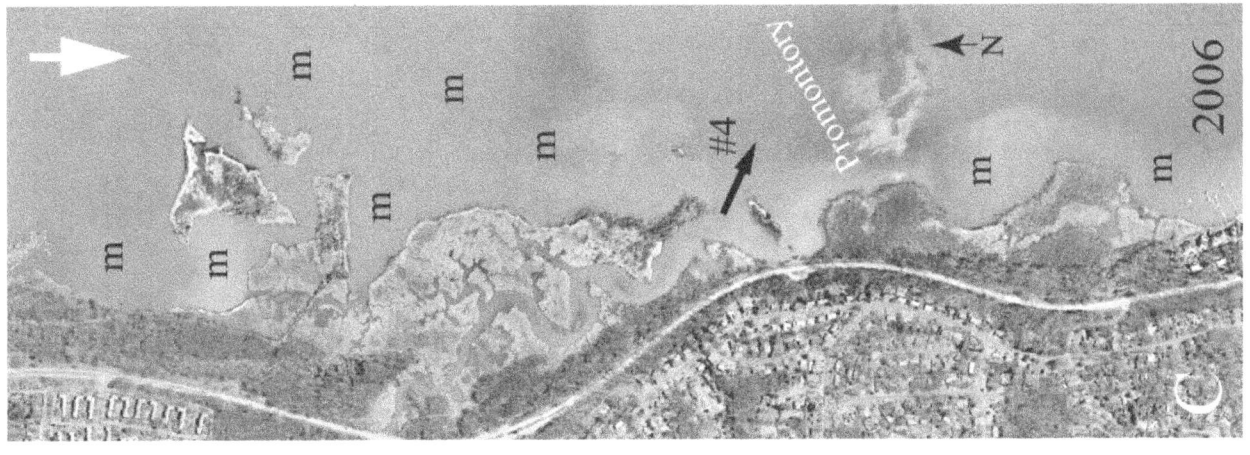

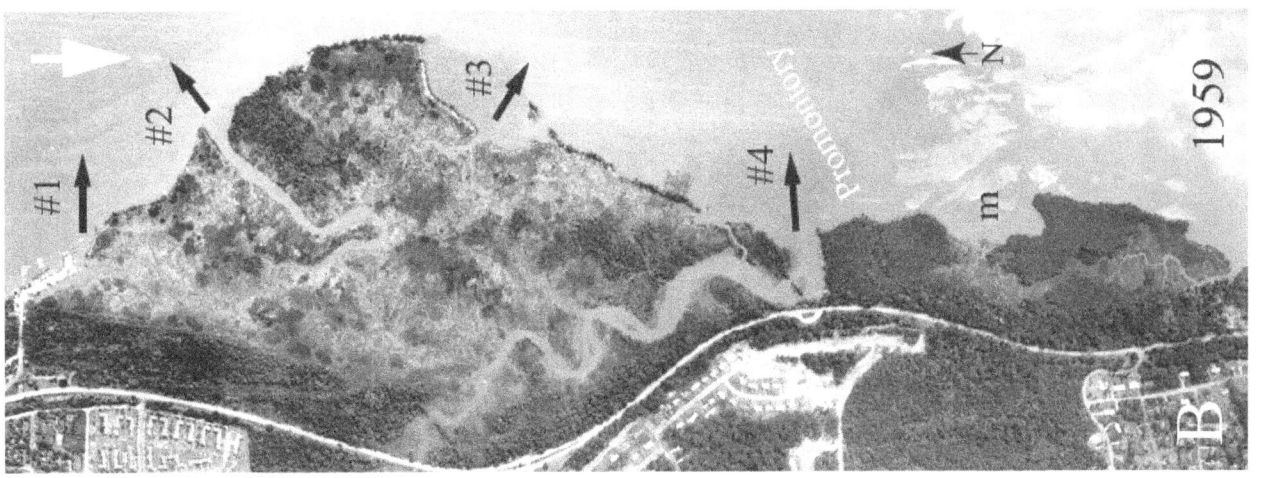

Figure 9. Comparison of tidal creek occurrence and outflow constraints with respect to Potomac River (A, 1937; B, 1959; and C, 2006). Areas mined out by Smoot Sand and Gravel are noted by the letter "m."

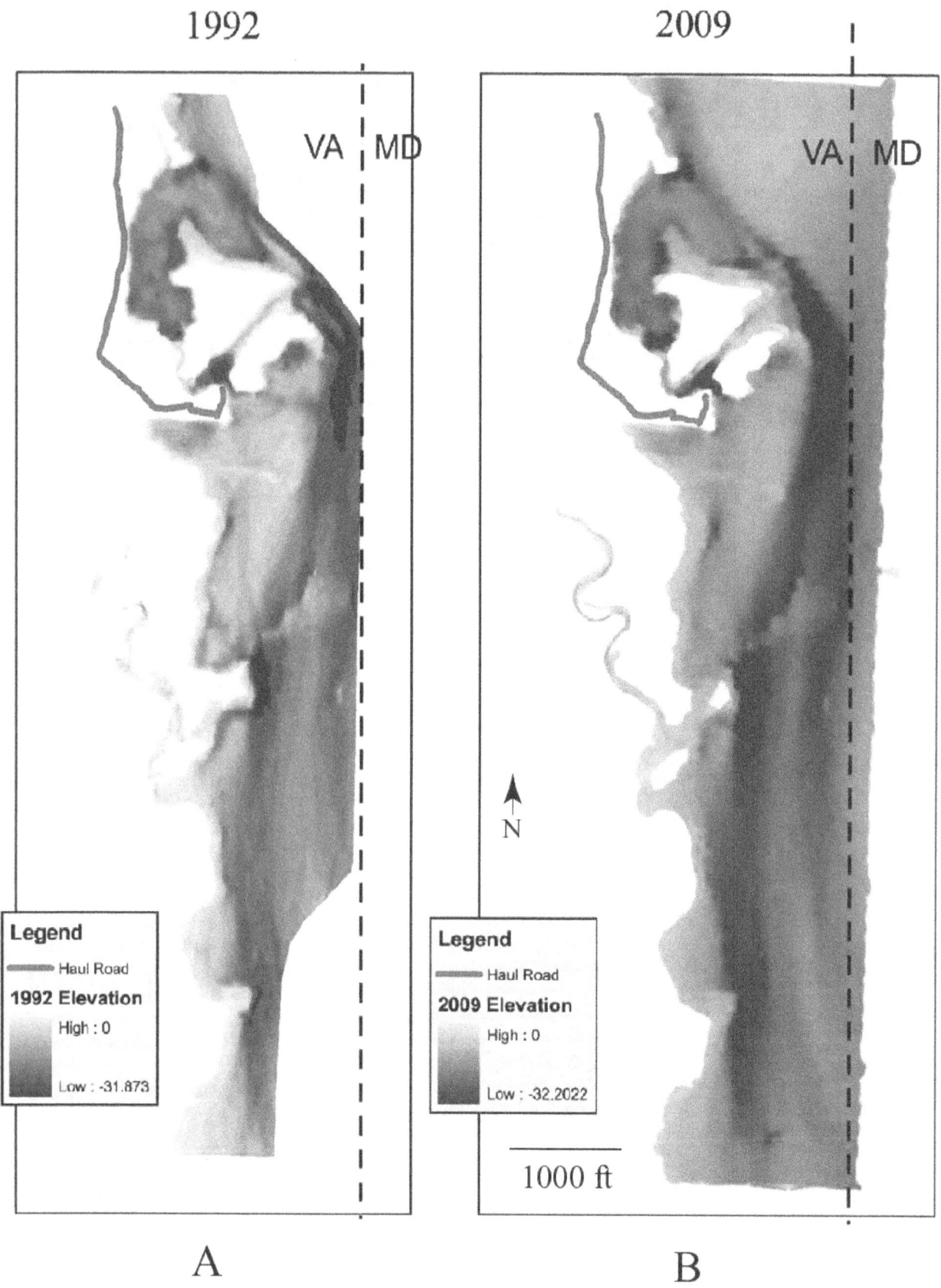

Figure 10.   Bathymetry, 1992 versus 2009 (source: National Park Service).

These two bathymetric surveys have been combined as a map product (Normandeau Associates, 2009; fig. 11). It classified Dyke Marsh into four color categories: white to denote terrestrial surface, red to denote presently submerged areas within the boundary that have accumulated sediment between 1992 and 2009 (shallowing river bottom), blue to denote presently submerged areas within the boundary that have lost sediment between 1992 and 2009 (deepening river bottom), and tan to denote areas that were "unmapped" in 1992. The incised channels (dark blue) show a pronounced widening and deepening by 2009, as noted above. The small peninsula on the original north shore of HIG (arrow) had been breached by 1992 (photo, fig. 11B). Field evidence suggests that the deconstruction of this small peninsula aided the aggressive westward erosion of the southern marsh's shoreline (the eastern edge of the HIG tidal creek network).

Initiation/Progression of East-West Marsh Loss along the Potomac's Western Shoreline

A primary goal of this study was to quantify accurately the recent rates of erosion on the marsh. One of the areas currently most affected is the present western shoreline of the Potomac River, where it abuts the eastern edge of the southern marsh (see white box, fig. 1). This north-to-south shoreline shows signs of severe westward erosion, toward the center of HIG. Three historical photographic images of the marsh were used to document this loss and (or) change of state (1987, 2002, 2006). These images were the basis for deriving initial quantitative estimates of shoreline erosion at Dyke Marsh over approximately two decades (19 years) and represented the best imagery available to us at the time. Erosion analysis using more recent imagery is ongoing, and its results will be presented elsewhere. Each photo recorded low tide conditions (~0–1.5 ft above mean low water).

We used commercially available software to overlay the photos accurately and to find fixed reference points (FRPs) that registered in all three images, as a prerequisite to quantifying shoreline loss.[9] Once the images were registered successfully in two dimensions, and placed into independent overlying transparent layers, we used FRPs east and west of the shoreline to define control lines along which shoreline positions could be measured for each year of imagery[10] (fig. 12A–C). It was necessary to obtain FRPs both east and west of the overall north-south shoreline transect that we were analyzing so that the shoreline positions at each station and the erosion estimates derived from them were interpolated accurately. In all cases our photographically derived distances were measured east to west along calibrated control lines ("subtransects").

The FRPs we selected included suburban landscape features west of the GWMP (for example, roof corners, sidewalk and street junctions, bridge abutments) and naturally occurring persistent features on the marsh proper (solitary tree profiles, stable tributary junctions, stable tree-throw). These have been identified by white squares with black centers on figure 12. Predominantly, the FRPs we identified were situated west of the shoreline transect because we were measuring shoreline loss against the eastern face of the marsh. To the east of the shoreline transect was only featureless open water of the Potomac River. We used a geometric construction to resolve this problem. Several FRPs did exist east of our north-south shoreline transect but were situated south of most of our target interval. We digitally projected a line northward and southward from one of those southerly FRPs, thereby establishing a north-south control line in mid-river (fig. 13; actually 2.5 degrees east of north). The natural marker (origin) for this north-south control line was a tree that originally bordered the dirt road atop the old earthen dike that ringed the perimeter of the marsh up to 1937 (figs. 13, 14A). Its standing dead trunk was stranded in situ out in the river just north of "Bird Island" in the 2006 imagery, marking the position of the old diked (dyke) road, and providing us with a critical easterly reference point. Once we established this mid-river north-south control line through "Bird Island," multiple stations could be constructed along a marsh shoreline transect by projecting east-west lines from individual FRPs (situated on and west of the marsh) eastward across the marsh, across the shoreline, to terminations at our mid-river north-south control line. Changes in shoreline positions on each year's image at each station then could be measured accurately as a proportion of two lines, each with predefined endpoints (AB/AC, fig. 14B), multiplied by a conversion factor to derive real footages. Line AC was the east-west control line of fixed length, determined independently at each station, that connected that station's FRP on the left (point A) to the north-south control line on the right (point C; that is, for all stations ST1 to ST30). The east-west control lines (AC) for a given station were identical among all of the three image years analyzed. In contrast, the line AB at each station differed in length each year, because it terminated at each year's independent position for the continuously shifting shoreline. Line AB connected the station FRP on the left (A) to the point of intersection (B) where it bisected the north-to-south shoreline in the photograph (at an intermediate point along AC). A schematic of this arrangement is shown in figure 14B, for a hypothetical station ("1Z") and a hypothetical north-south control line. Our stations for measurement were labeled north to south, from station ST1 to station ST30 (fig. 13). At each station, the proportion AB/AC could be converted to real footages using an external calibration line XY, taken along a residential street segment visible in all three photos (fig. 12C). The photo calibration line XY and its actual ground distance defined the conversion factor necessary to transpose photo line lengths into accurate field footages at each station (to calculate true distances from the FRP at each station to its shoreline intersection). Our calibration line

---

[9] This imagery was not geo-referenced Tiff imagery, and therefore we did not use GIS as the tool of preference to analyze our photo series.

[10] From the FRP eastward to the point of intersection where the eroded shoreline bisected the horizontal control line.

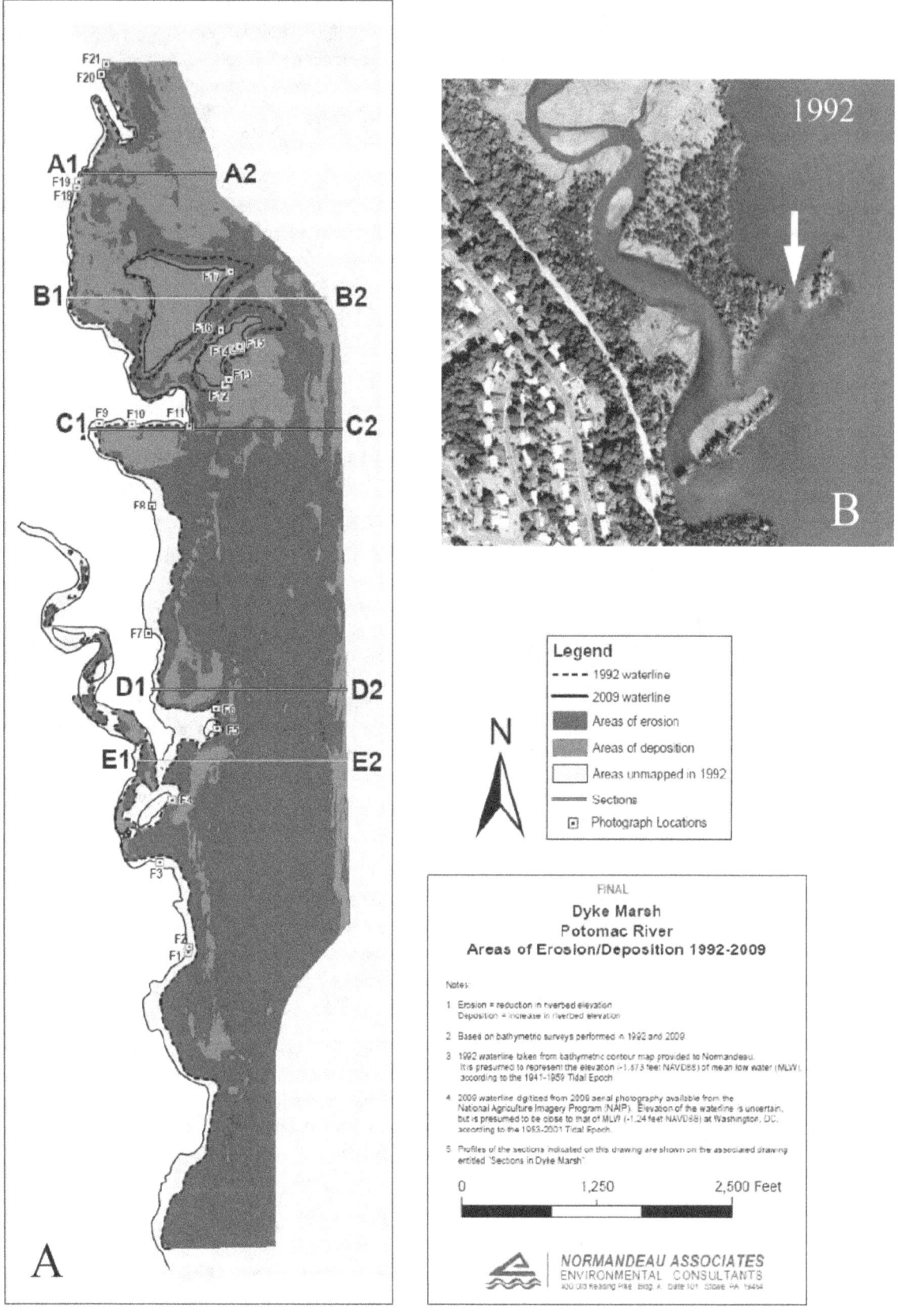

Figure 11.   Synthesis of (A) 1992 and 2009 bathymetry (Normandeau Associates, 2009) and (B) 1992 aerial photo of peninsula, showing its disintegration by storms by 1992. The "Photograph Locations" symbols noted in the legend and in figure 11A refer only to the 2009 report (not this study).

Figure 12A. Southern marsh aerial photographs showing fixed reference points (FRPs) identified in this report for calculations of shoreface erosion: 1987. Note red and white field calibration line (laser measured at 165 m ± 1 m) to southwest of marsh (see fig. 12C).

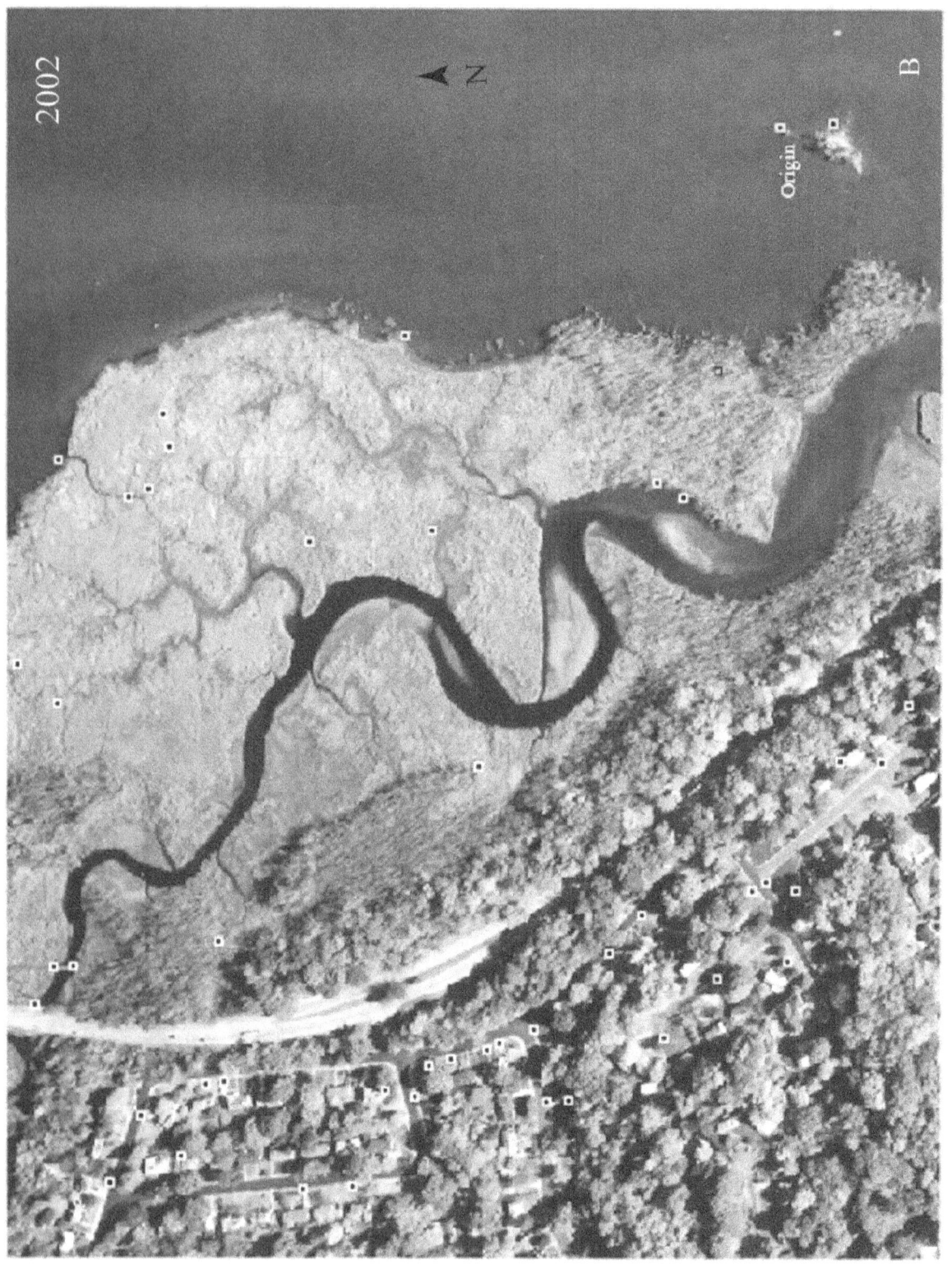

Figure 12B.   Southern marsh aerial photographs showing fixed reference points (FRPs) identified in this report for calculations of shoreface erosion: 2002. Note red and white field calibration line (laser measured at 165 m ± 1 m) to southwest of marsh (see fig. 12C).

Figure 12C. Southern marsh aerial photographs showing fixed reference points (FRPs) identified in this report for calculations of shoreface erosion: 2006. Note red and white field calibration line (laser measured at 165 m ± 1 m) to southwest of marsh.

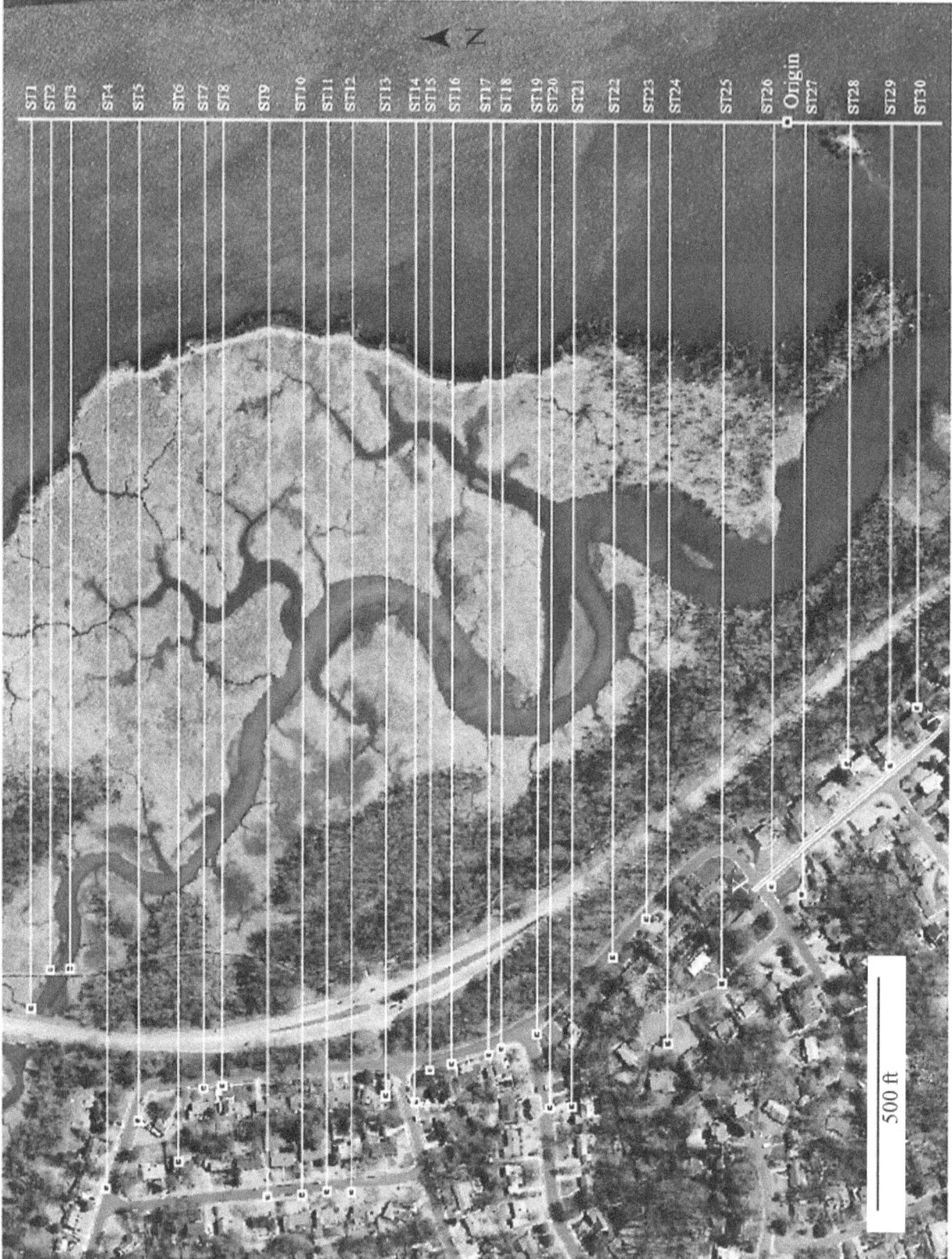

Figure 13. Control lines (subtransects ST1–ST30) for calculating shoreline loss. Note north-south termination line projecting through stranded tree (origin) just north of "Bird Island."

distance was documented at 165 m ± 1 m by a laser range-finding binocular and white reflective board. This photo-based line length of XY is given in table 3, along with its conversion factor, all line lengths, and converted ground distances, per year of record. Shoreline loss was calculated in feet by solving the equation:

$$L = [(AB_{T2} - AB_{T1})/AC]*(AC*n),$$

where

AB_{T2}	=	the photo distance from point A to point B for the more recent year (T2),
AB_{T1}	=	the photo distance from point A to point B for the less recent year (T1),
AC	=	the photo distance of the horizontal control line from point A to point C (that is, terminating at the north-south control line and identical in length for T1 and T2),
n	=	the conversion factor defined by line EF (expressed as footage per photo distance), and
L	=	the linear erosion (in feet) occurring between time 2 (T2) and time 1 (T1).

The linear shoreline loss results (east-to-west, per time interval, per station) are found in table 3 and figure 15.

Figure 15 summarizes the linear shoreline loss estimates along our north-south transect for two time intervals, 1987 to 2002 and 2002 to 2006. The x-axis represents the cumulative linear distance along the photo transect (station by station), and the y-axis represents the linear shoreline loss at that station during each of the two time intervals. The average annual shoreline loss rates observed for the 1987 to 2002 interval were 1.13 ft$_{min}$ (6.05 ft$_{mean}$) 8.08 ft$_{max}$. Average annual shoreline loss rates observed for the 2002 to 2006 time interval were 1.77 ft$_{min}$ (7.81 ft$_{mean}$) 28.16 ft$_{max}$. Seventy-five percent of the stations we measured experienced a cumulative linear shoreline loss of over 90 ft during this 19-year interval (fig. 16).

These shoreline loss rates can be put into local geological context by comparing them to direct cliff-face erosion rates measured at 13 stations along the shoreline (cliff face) at the Elizabeth Hartwell Mason Neck National Wildlife Refuge (hereafter designated MNWR), ~11.5 miles south and west of Dyke Marsh. Two years of observational data (1995 and 1996) provided to us by the U.S. Fish and Wildlife Service (USFWS) indicated that the average minimum, mean, maximum annual footage loss rates observed at MNWR--0.71 ft$_{min}$ (2.12 ft$_{mean}$) 3.75 ft$_{max}$--were less than half the amount of the 15-year annual loss values calculated for Dyke Marsh (data source: D. Melvin, USFWS, internal memo, 1996; table 4). Figure 17 compares the average erosion rates (minimum, mean, maximum) at MNWR for 1995 and 1996 to the 1987 to 2002 and 2002 to 2006 erosion estimates at Dyke Marsh (this study). Loss rates were higher at Dyke Marsh than at MNWR, and the 2002 to 2006 time interval showed loss rates that were notably higher than the 15-year interval preceding it. Visual inspection of 2007 and 2009 imagery of Dyke Marsh that

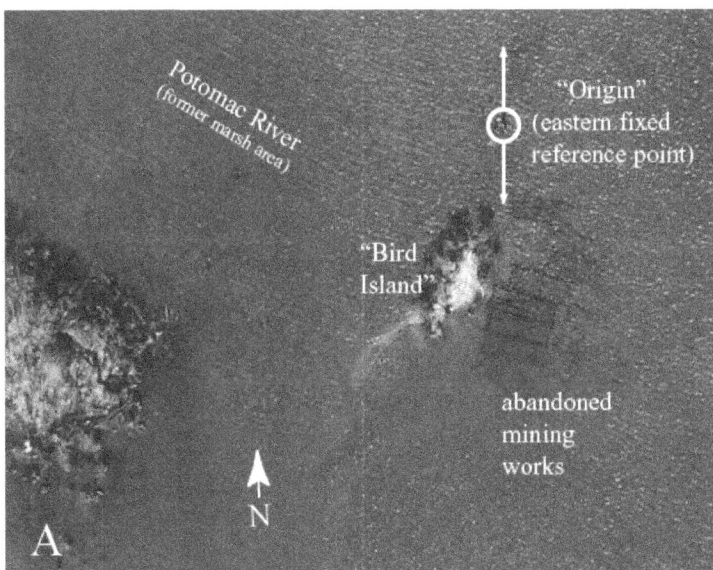

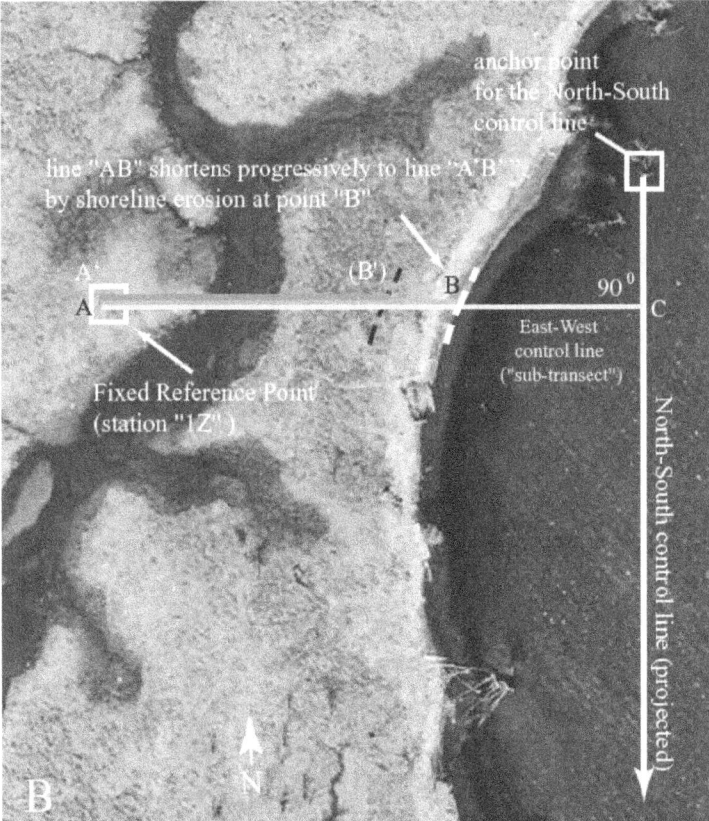

Figure 14. A, Close up of "origin" point for north-south termination line. B, Schematic of shoreline loss estimation.

Table 3.   Transect-based shoreline erosion estimates for Dyke Marsh (1987–2002).

Station	Line length (in feet[1])			Linear feet of loss (erosion)			N-S distance (feet)	Interval (From >To)	Shoreline loss (square feet)		
	1985	2002	2006	1985–2002	2002–2006	1985–2006			1987–2002	2002–2006	1987–2006
1	1132.3	1115.3	1094.0	17.1	21.2	38.3	0.0				
2	1103.3	1069.2	1045.1	34.0	24.1	58.1	43.3	ST1 >ST2	1105.3	979.9	2085.2
3	1268.5	1182.8	1139.6	85.7	43.3	129.0	87.9	ST2 >ST3	2673.3	1503.4	4176.7
4	1835.9	1765.7	1747.3	70.1	18.4	88.6	169.4	ST3 >ST4	6346.9	2513.5	8860.4
5	1691.3	1621.9	1607.1	69.4	14.9	84.2	240.6	ST4 >ST5	4964.6	1185.2	6149.8
6	1818.6	1747.0	1720.1	71.6	26.9	98.5	330.2	ST5 >ST6	6317.2	1872.8	8190.0
7	1703.4	1628.3	1594.2	75.1	34.0	109.1	387.6	ST6 >ST7	4208.5	1749.5	5958.0
8	1717.3	1638.6	1596.8	78.7	41.8	120.5	428.3	ST7 >ST8	3131.9	1544.3	4676.2
9	1981.1	1898.2	1864.9	82.9	33.3	116.2	529.6	ST8 >ST9	8185.9	3803.5	11989.4
10	1964.6	1888.7	1851.2	75.8	37.5	113.4	608.3	ST9 >ST10	6246.3	2787.6	9033.9
11	1919.7	1855.2	1834.7	64.5	20.5	85.0	663.9	ST10 >ST11	3899.9	1613.0	5512.9
12	1925.6	1866.8	1828.6	58.9	38.2	97.1	720.5	ST11 >ST12	3493.4	1662.3	5155.7
13	1698.6	1619.3	1600.2	79.3	19.1	98.4	797.1	ST12 >ST13	5290.4	2193.6	7484.0
14	1694.9	1589.3	1577.3	105.6	12.0	117.6	861.6	ST13 >ST14	5963.7	1002.7	6966.4
15	1564.9	1509.4	1487.5	55.5	22.0	77.4	896.3	ST14 >ST15	2794.3	589.0	3383.3
16	1584.6	1486.8	1462.0	97.8	24.8	122.6	946.5	ST15 >ST16	3853.1	1175.9	5029.0
17	1543.2	1473.8	1448.3	69.4	25.5	94.9	1029.5	ST16 >ST17	6931.9	2088.4	9020.2
18	1528.6	1468.4	1433.7	60.2	34.7	94.9	1058.9	ST17 >ST18	1904.5	885.1	2789.6
19	1562.2	1453.8	1412.6	108.4	41.1	149.5	1137.1	ST18 >ST19	6600.5	2968.0	9568.5
20	1715.5	1612.7	1585.7	102.8	26.9	129.7	1166.5	ST19 >ST20	3102.6	1000.2	4102.8
21	1735.9	1614.8	1607.7	121.1	7.1	128.2	1215.4	ST20 >ST21	5473.7	832.1	6305.8
22	1380.5	1323.8	1312.5	56.7	11.3	68.1	1305.8	ST21 >ST22	8035.8	833.5	8869.3
23	1296.6	1223.0	1142.7	73.6	80.3	153.9	1379.8	ST22 >ST23	4825.5	3393.2	8218.7
24	1545.6	1445.0	1423.2	100.6	21.8	122.4	1429.0	ST23 >ST24	4286.9	2513.1	6799.9
25	1421.8	1318.4	1305.4	103.4	13.1	116.5	1549.1	ST24 >ST25	12246.3	2092.5	14338.8
26	1213.0	1113.1	1018.9	99.9	94.2	194.1	1659.6	ST25 >ST26	11236.2	5927.1	17163.3
27	1251.1	1140.6	1027.9	110.5	112.6	223.2	1738.6	ST26 >ST27	8313.5	8171.6	16485.2
28	1373.7	976.2	960.6	397.5	15.6	413.1	1836.1	ST27 >ST28	24757.2	6249.0	31006.1
29	1129.5	1026.7	1013.5	102.8	13.2	116.0	1928.2	ST28 >ST29	23031.7	1326.5	24358.2
30	954.5	859.5	851.9	94.9	7.6	102.5	1989.1	ST29 >ST30	6027.3	634.6	6661.9
								Total Sq.Ft.	195248.1	65091.1	260339.2
								Total Acres	4.5	1.5	6.0

Photo calibration		
Photo length (in.)	Laser distance	Inches/foot (photo)
0.6632	541.34 ft	0.001225
	(165 m ± 1 m)	

[1] from fixed reference point to termination

Linear shoreline loss per station at Dyke Marsh
(1987–2002 versus 2002–2006)

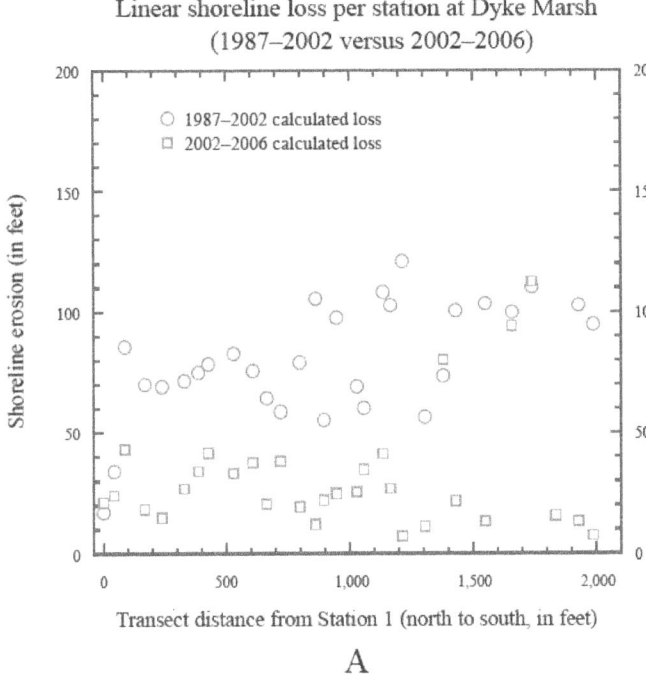

A

Linear shoreline loss per year at Dyke Marsh (1987–2006)

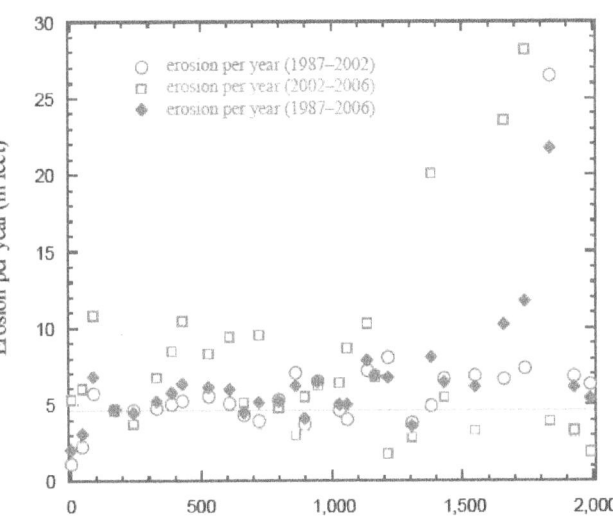

B

Figure 15. Linear shoreline loss results. A, Linear shoreline loss per station at Dyke Marsh (1987–2002 versus 2002–2006). B, Linear shoreline loss per year at Dyke Marsh (1987–2006). Loss is recorded per station (ST1–ST30) in three ways: average annual loss between 1987 and 2002, average annual loss between 2002 and 2006, and combined average annual loss between 1987 and 2006.

Cumulative shoreline loss at Dyke Marsh (1987–2006)

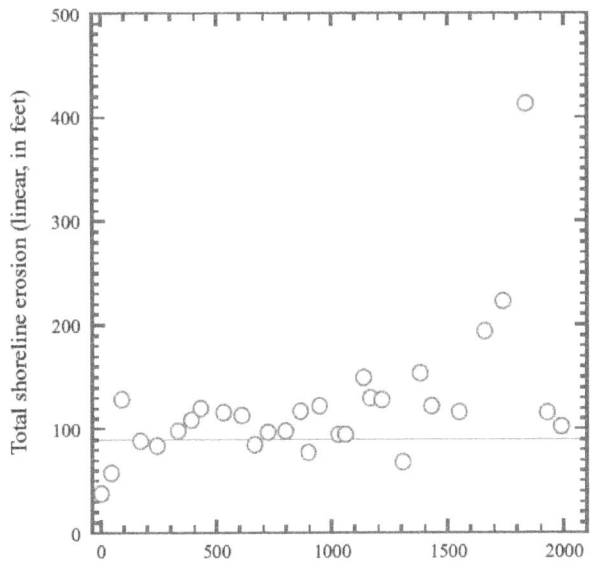

Transect distance from Station 1 (north to south, in feet)

Figure 16. Cumulative shoreline loss at Dyke Marsh (1987–2006). Loss is linear, per station (ST1–ST30). Note extreme loss (~400 ft) as an artifact of peninsular breach. More than 75 percent of the stations displayed east-west linear shoreline loss of 90 ft (red line) or greater during this time interval.

Table 4. Cliff-face (shoreline) loss at Elizabeth Hartwell Mason Neck National Wildlife Refuge, 1995–1996[1].

Stake	Start distance (feet)	Distance 1995 (feet)	Distance 1996 (feet)	Shore loss 1995 (feet)	Shore loss 1996 (feet)	Total linear loss (feet)
1	50.00	47.25	47.25	2.75	0.00	2.75
2	50.00	49.17	46.83	0.83	2.34	3.17
3	50.00	49.58	43.00	0.42	6.58	7.00
4	50.00	50	48.58	0.00	1.42	1.42
5	50.00	46.42	44.58	3.58	1.84	5.42
6	50.00	49.58	43.83	0.42	5.75	6.17
7	50.00	48.5	47.25	1.50	1.25	2.75
8	50.00	50.00	50.00	L[2]	L[2]	indeterminate
9	50.00	48.17	42.50	1.83	5.67	7.50
10	50.00	45.50	L[2]	4.50	L[2]	indeterminate
11	50.00	49.50	48.00	0.50	1.50	2.00
12	50.00	48.67	L[2]	1.33	L[2]	indeterminate
13	50.00	47.92	L[2]	2.08	L[2]	indeterminate

[1] Data Source: U.S. Fish and Wildlife Service

[2] L=loss of calibration stake (no measurement)

Minimum, mean, and maximum rates of annual shoreline loss
at Dyke Marsh, versus annual loss rates at Mason Neck Wildlife Refuge

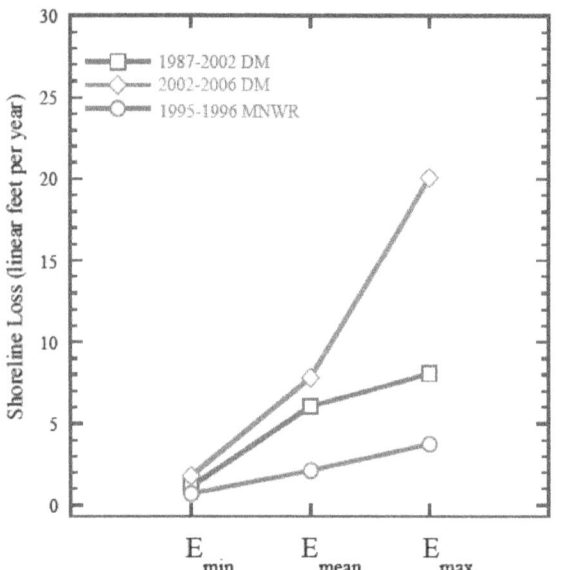

Figure 17.   Minimum, mean, and maximum rates of annual shoreline loss at Dyke Marsh, versus annual loss rate at Elizabeth Hartwell Mason Neck Wildlife Refuge. Dyke Marsh loss is linear, and represents annual rates from two time intervals (1987–2002, 2002–2006), compared to average cliff-face loss rates at the heron rookery at Elizabeth Hartwell Mason Neck National Wildlife Refuge (MNWR, 1995–1996).

we recently acquired suggests that the marsh continued to experience moderate to strong erosion after 2006 (fig. 18). Quantitative estimates of shoreline loss between 2006 and 2009 are pending.

We converted linear shoreline loss into acreage loss at Dyke Marsh by multiplying the north-south field distance between successive horizontal control lines (transect stations) times the average of the combined footage losses at each of the two adjacent stations (table 3). The square footage of all "loss" subplots was totaled, then converted to total acreage (at 43,560 ft^2 per acre). Our analyses indicate that from 1987 to 2002, ~4.48 acres of marsh were lost to shoreline erosion between stations ST1 and ST30. This represents ~10.3 percent of the original 1987 central parcel acreage (~43.33 acres, table 2). From 2002 to 2006 ~1.49 acres were lost to shoreline erosion between these same stations. That represents ~3.4 percent of the original 1987 central parcel acreage. In total, we estimate that more than 13.5 percent of the central parcel of the marsh was destroyed by shoreline erosion along the Potomac River over a span of 19 years. This loss represents more than 7.5 percent of the entire marsh (per its 1987 acreage), without including estimates of the visible loss in the marsh parcels north and south of our study area. Detailed shoreline loss rates have not yet been analyzed north of station ST1 or south of station ST30; our calculations suggest that shoreline erosion between ST1 and ST30 accounts for ~30 to 50 percent of all marsh acreage lost annually.

Piracy of Distal Tidal Creek Tributaries and Foreshortening of Tidal Creek Network

A significant consequence of this shoreline erosion is the lateral piracy of higher order tidal tributaries of the HIG by the Potomac River. Storm waves have breached and presently are continuing to breach distal tidal tributaries of HIG, creating riverine cut-through channels that now bypass the formerly readjusted (1959) position for the mouth of HIG. Aerial imagery from 2006 and 2009 and field imagery from April 2010 illustrate the progression of one of these breaches (fig. 18). This distal tributary had not been fully breached and scoured of vegetation in spring 2006 or spring 2009 (fig. 18A, B) but had been so by April 2010 (fig. 18C). Additionally, the 2009 tropical storm season was relatively quiet at Dyke Marsh; therefore, one or several nor'easters (winter storms) have been implicated as the most probable cause of this breach. The strongest nor'easters to approach Dyke Marsh over this period were the remnant of Hurricane Ida (November 2009), the "Blizzard of 2009" (December 2009), and the storm of February 2010 (see appendix 5). It is likely that one or more of these storms induced wave erosion that ultimately caused the breach illustrated in figure 18.

Existing cross-cutting tidal creeks just landward of these captured distal tributaries (especially those whose axis runs subperpendicular to shoreline) likely will be widened, deepened, and "blown out" by successive storm wave action, as has happened previously on the marsh (fig. 18). We have documented this in cross-cutting tidal creeks farther south (creek axis X–Y, fig. 18D–F). This particular stream piracy ultimately created "Angel Island" and "Bird Island" from what was once continuous marshland. The results of such sequential piracies are threefold: Potomac River water at rising tide bypasses the long travel path up the gut into the marsh's most distant tributaries, the foreshortening of HIG requires it to readjust its stream profile and flow velocities, and damaging wave energy is delivered incrementally deeper into the marsh during storms. The ultimate result of this repeated reduction of travel path for the water exchange is that the effective mouth of HIG is migrating headward (deeper into the remnant marsh) as distal tidal tributaries are breached and widened by wave action. The history of this headward retreat is diagrammed in figure 19.

Physical Habitat Fragmentation

We predict (on the basis of historical precedent at Dyke Marsh) that continued and persistent inward and northward migration of the functional mouth of the HIG tidal creek will leave a fragmented series of marsh islands south of the retreating tidal creek mouth, where originally there was intact marsh. Such a result will have biological impacts. First, this study confirms that substantial amounts of marsh habitat are being destroyed directly by persistent shoreline erosion.

Second, habitat connectivity is being reduced concurrently for terrestrial marsh-dwelling species, as a consequence of this stream piracy. We estimate that as much as 40 percent of the presently intact southern part of the tidal marsh (that part now fed by HIG) faces an imminent loss of connectivity (fig. 20). Included among the species which likely will be

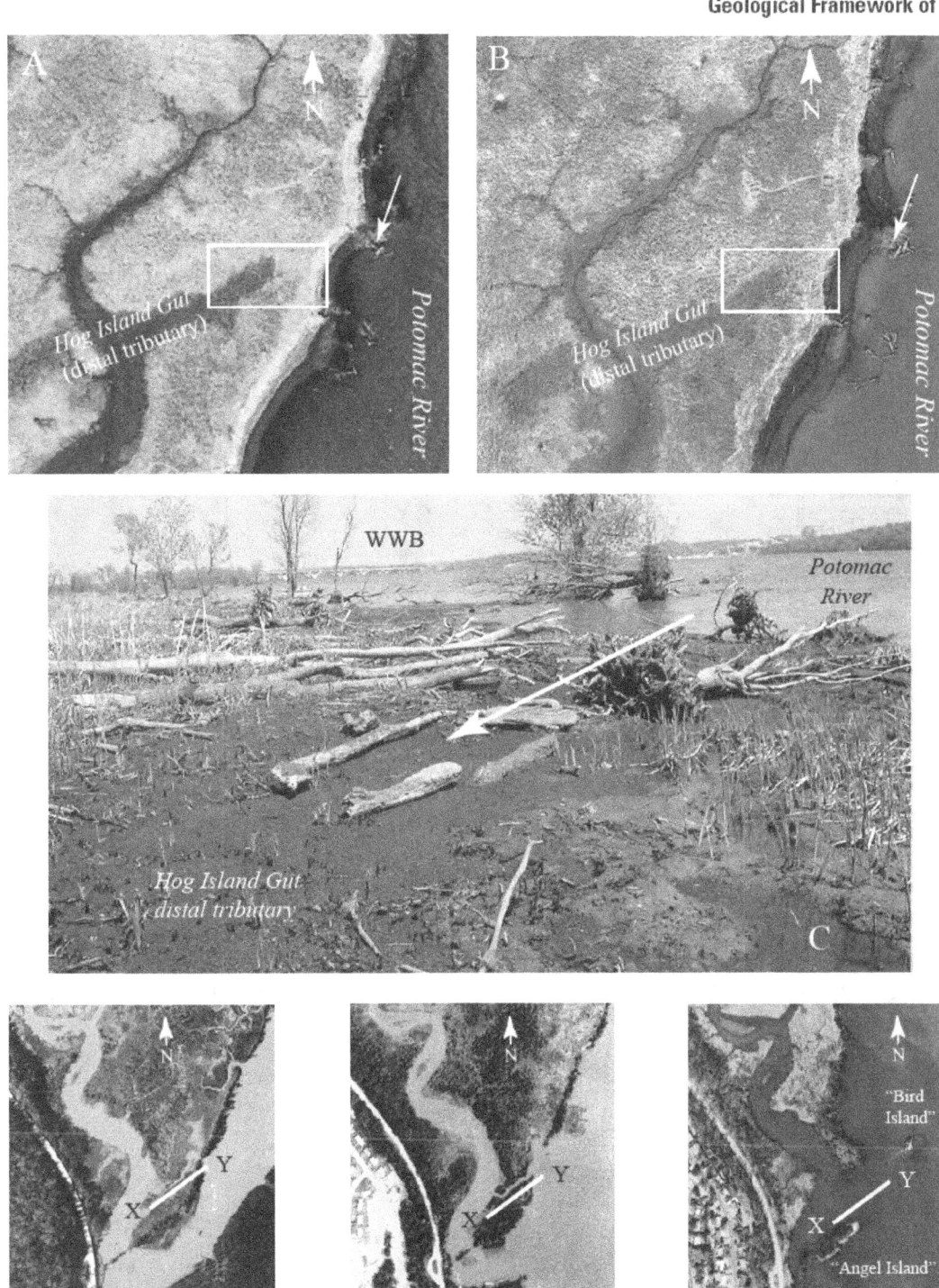

Figure 18. Breach of Hog Island Gut tributaries, past and present. A, Aerial imagery (2006) of southern marsh breach site showing extreme shoreface erosion but no breach (vegetation stripping). Site located just south of NPS stationary elevation table (SET station). White arrow notes stationary treefall for reference. B, Aerial imagery (2009) (source: Virginia Base Map Survey, 2010) showing the same feature. Vegetation band still present between distal tributary of Hog Island Gut and Potomac River, but narrower. C, April 2010 field photo showing evidence of full breach of tributary. Potomac storm waves have carried trees, logs, tires and other debris shoreward, tearing up the organic marsh mat that previously separated the Potomac River and Hog Island Gut. The Woodrow Wilson Bridge (WWB) is visible in the background (southernmost point along Washington Beltway, I-495). Photo credit: J.P. Smoot. D, Aerial photo (1937) showing unnamed east-west tidal creek at original meander near the mouth of Hog Island Gut (marked as line X–Y). E, Same tidal creek in 1959 aerial photo, showing evidence of channel widening and marsh shoreface erosion by storm waves (at point Y). F, Former 1937 tidal creek position on 2006 aerial photo, showing two small erosional island remnants ("Angel Island" and "Bird Island") where previously there was fast land.

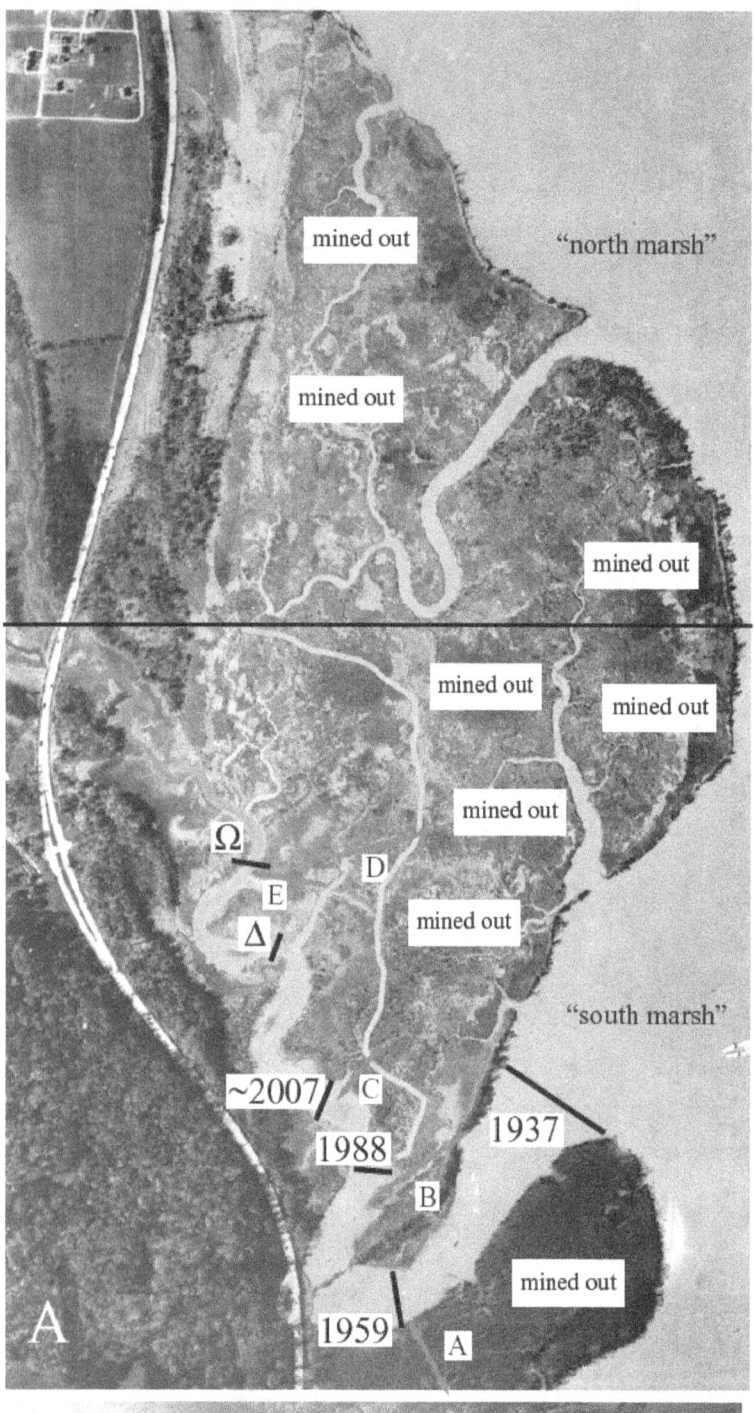

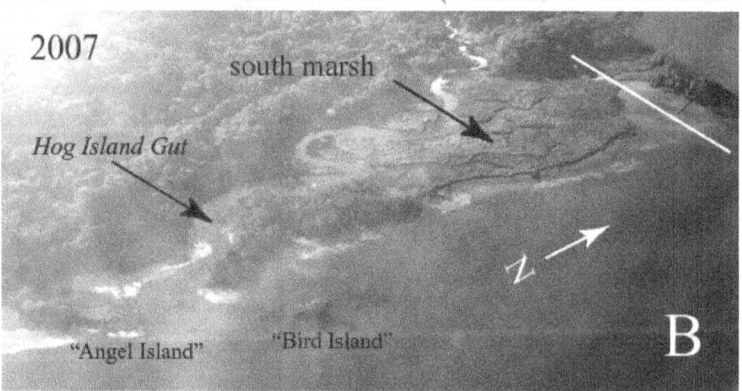

Figure 19. A, Diagram of the progressive northwestward migration of the terminal outflow point of Hog Island Gut (HIG), from 1937 to 2009. Consecutive positions of the mouth of HIG are marked by black lines perpendicular to the channel axis. Horizontal black line shows northern limit of "south marsh" as used in this study. Irregular north-to-south blue line traces the approximate position of the 2006 shoreline in the south marsh. Removal of the promontory (A) shortened the length of HIG back to the 1959 position. Storm breach of the tidal creek at "B" shortened the HIG back to the 1988 position. Storm waves from Hurricane Isabel (2003) and possibly Hurricane Charley (2004) likely contributed to breach at "C," and shortened HIG back to approximately the 2007 position. Breach observed in figure 18 is at position "D," and has begun to erode by April 2010. This effectively will shorten the HIG back to position "Δ" with successive erosion at position "D." The tidal creek at "E" would be among the next successive storm failures, and analogous to the blow-out by storm waves seen in figure 18D–F. This ultimately will shorten the HIG back to position "Ω." B, Oblique aerial photo of south marsh for comparison to original marsh extent in figure 19A. The white line on the right of the photo marks the boundary between the south marsh (to left) and the north marsh (to right). Airplane wing blocks part of north marsh view (upper right corner). Photo credit: J.E. Repetski.

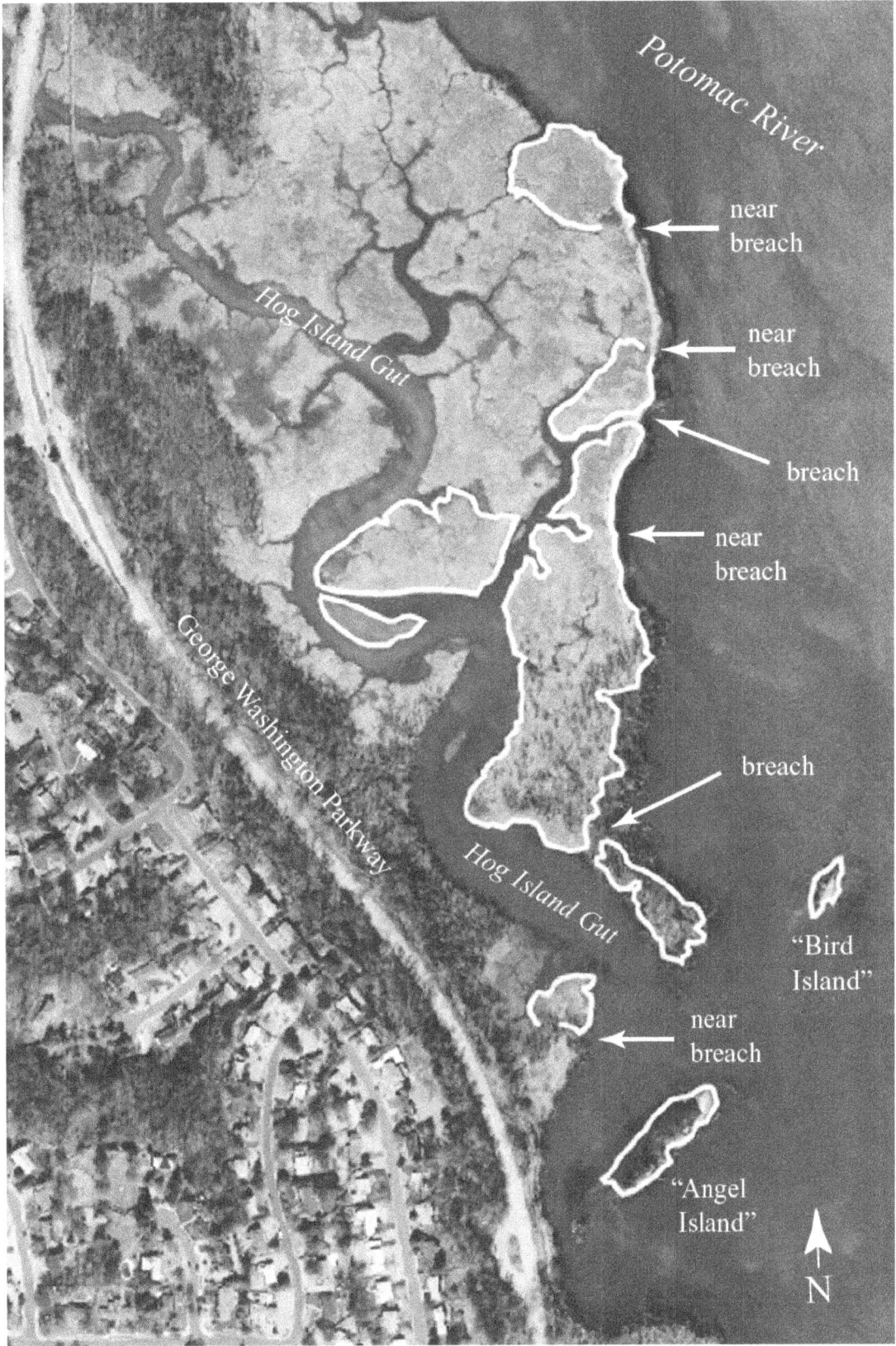

Figure 20.   Aerial photo (2006) of southern marsh, showing the positions of breaches and near-breaches along the eastern shoreface. Unchecked storm erosion is progressively fragmenting and diminishing marsh acreage (habitat) in the southern marsh. Parcels of marsh that are becoming progressively more insular are highlighted with a white lined border.

adversely affected by habitat fragmentation are the Red-wing Blackbird (*Agelaius phoeniceus*) and Marsh Wren (*Cistotho-rus palustris*). Tidal channel edges are the preferred nesting habitat for marsh wren; this is also where erosion evidence is observed. Spencer (2000) has noted that suitable wren nesting habitat already is quite limited on the marsh, with nesting wrens crowding into a progressively diminishing area. She calculated that suitable wren habitat comprises ~12 percent of the main marsh. She also calculated that suitable nesting terri-tory forms only a third of that parcel, so that suitable nesting sites comprise only ~3.6 percent of the marsh. Storm erosion continues to diminish that habitat.

Characterizing Present Processes Operating on the Marsh

Relative Effect of Constructive Versus Destructive Geologic Processes on Marsh

We have documented more than half a millennium of sedi-mentation on the north marsh. Figure 21 illustrates our prelimi-nary pollen analysis from core DM1, a push-core taken on the northern end of "Dyke Island." The Accelerator Mass Spec-trometry radiocarbon age we derived from organics sampled near the marsh's base (~162 centimeters (cm) depth) indicates

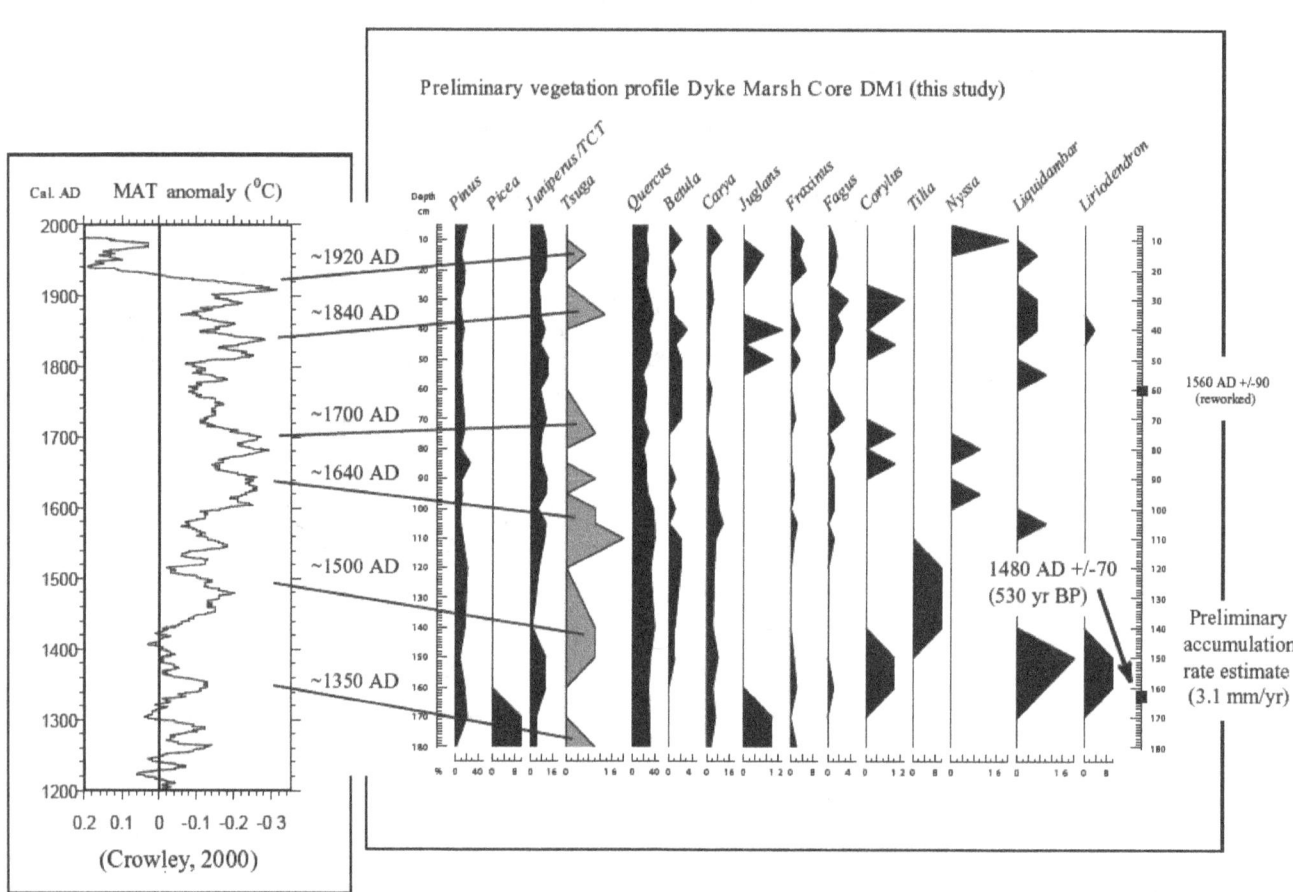

Figure 21.   Preliminary pollen diagram from northern marsh, Dyke Island (core DM1). This vertical sequence documents the terrestrial vegetation historically surrounding the marsh. Spikes in the hemlock pollen downcore are tentatively correlated to previously documented regional cold pulses in the mean annual temperature (MAT) of the Northern Hemisphere over the past millennium (Crowley, 2000). Based on this initial paleoclimate correlation and our radiometric date at ~162 cm core depth, we infer nearly continuous sedimentation at this site over the past ~500 years, during both warm and cool climate intervals. The average accumulation rate appears to be ~3.1 mm/yr at this site.

an age of ~1480 A.D. ± 70 yr (this study, table 1). This defines an average sediment accumulation rate of ~3.06 millimeters per year (mm/yr) for the marsh at this depth. Abundance spikes in pollen from hemlock (*Tsuga canadensis*), a cold-tolerant tree found in core sediments above 160 cm, are here tentatively correlated to the historic cold pulses in Northern Hemisphere climate over the past millennium, per Crowley (2000). Our preliminary analyses indicate that the marsh accumulated sediments persistently through this time interval, through periods of both cool and warm climate. The accumulation rate derived from the basal radiometric date in the southern marsh suggests that Dyke Marsh's accumulation rate in places may have been as high as ~5.25 mm/yr (table 1). The accumulation rate results presented here are preliminary; our ongoing fieldwork is focused on establishing accumulation rates along multiple transects across the marsh, in order to constrain Dyke Marsh's historic accumulation rates more conclusively.

However, evidence of destructive geological processes also are present at the marsh, even as it has been accumulating sediment persistently. Photographic and field evidence illustrates that storm waves episodically deposit a dense mantle of "debris throw" (logs, discarded plastic, tires) 10 to 15 ft into the outer edge of the eastern marsh, while simultaneously tearing apart the existing marsh vegetation behind it (riverward). The "rip-up" zone appears to be a result of effective translocation of wave energy now shoaling directly at the marsh's edge (fig. 22), where it depletes its energy by vertically scouring the marsh. This scour and debris-throw combination is a relatively new phase in the increasing wave-dominance on the marsh shoreline. Scour and debris throw do not appear to be as well developed in earlier aerial photos as in later ones (compare fig. 12A and 12C; see also fig. 18A). Previously this shoreline area was well protected from wind-driven waves by the promontory that formed HIG's southern embankment (fig. 2), until the initial phases of dredge mining removed it, and the protection it afforded, in the late 1930s to early 1940s. The southern shoreline area was protected to a lesser extent subsequently by a small peninsula which existed on the northern side of the HIG terminal outflow. That peninsula was breached by wave erosion from the south by 1992 (fig. 11B).

The combination of debris throw and marsh scouring is visually striking in the field. The scour is effective in stripping away the dense marsh root mat on which the emergent marsh vegetation grows, fully exposing the inorganic sediments that underlie the marsh (fig. 22E). The scouring at the river edge is deep, with cuspate pits, and exposes the contact between the organic-rich marsh sediments and the organic-poor, pre-marsh sediments beneath. Our Eijelkamp manual sidewall corer most frequently penetrated this contact at approximately 1.4 to 1.5 m (4.6 ft–4.9 ft) below ground surface across the marsh, thus documenting a maximum possible depth for this shoreline wave scour.

Unconstrained storm erosion has degraded the health of the marsh woodland and in many places is deconstructing the woodland. Waves have exposed entire root systems of mature trees along the eastern shoreline as they erode the marsh edge.

Tree root systems are being exhumed by waves, undercut, and then ultimately toppled and killed in place by continued wave action (figs. 18, 22). A minimum scour depth along the marsh edge is constrained by the exhumed in situ tree rootballs at the marsh shoreline. The vertical exposure of in situ tree roots at the current marsh edge documents that this scour is at least ~45 to 60 cm deep (18–24 inches, fig. 22C). Our aerial photographic evidence suggests that a widespread recent destruction of marsh woodland occurred between 2002 and 2006 (See "Continuous Versus Discontinuous Erosion Events").

Relative Effect of River Flooding Versus Wave Action on Marsh Loss

In our initial examination of erosional features in the marsh, we looked for evidence of river flow erosion from flooding of the Potomac River. We predicted asymmetric distribution of sediment accumulation of coarse sediment upflow of obstacles such as trees, rocks, or manmade structures, and erosional pockets on the downflow side that would be filled with finer grained sediment. We also expected to see stacking of pebbles and cobbles such that they were systematically inclined upflow (imbrication). At a larger scale, we predicted that erosional patterns would produce spindle-shaped remnant patches of marsh that are elongate parallel to the river flow direction. None of these features were observed. Instead, we saw abundant evidence of wave erosion and sediment transport. We noted that trees and other debris were oriented with long axes parallel to shorelines, in places perpendicular to the main river channel. We also noted flat-topped sediment ridges continuous along the shoreline with steeply dipping faces landward. These features are consistent with wave washover during storms. Rootballs of trees were systematically eroded on the river side with no asymmetry parallel to river flow. Pebbles and cobbles were imbricated with dips away from land, indicating net transport perpendicular to river flow. At a large scale, erosion patterns are in the form of cuspate pockets, which are most pronounced on the southern and southeastern faces of the marsh. The sequential photographs for 1987 through 2002 show that erosion was primarily on the southern side of the marsh by deepening of the cusps until blocks of marsh were isolated. These data indicate that most of the ongoing erosion is due to wave action rather than river flooding.

We obtained a preliminary assessment of how much wave energy could be produced by wind blowing along the Potomac River by determining the maximum effective fetch for the southern end of the marsh. The technique we used was derived empirically by the U.S. Army Corps of Engineers (U.S. Army Coastal Engineering Research Center, 1972). The effective fetch measures the effect of the geometry of the water body on the size of waves formed by a sustained wind blowing across the surface at a given direction. We were interested in the maximum wave power, so we measured the maximum linear fetch, then the fetch along 6-degree rays from that line on each side for 42 degrees (fig. 23) (Hakanson and Jansson, 1983, p. 189–190). The effective fetch is provided by the equation:

$$F = \frac{\sum x_i \cdot \cos \lambda_i}{\sum \cos \lambda_i} \qquad (1)$$

where

F is the effective fetch,

x_i is the linear fetch along ray i, and

λ_i is the angle of the ray i from the maximum linear fetch.

A narrow body of water such as the Potomac River near Dyke Marsh will provide a substantially smaller effective fetch than the greatest linear fetch. Given the effective fetch, there is a unique Airy wave (simple sinusoidal wave) that will form under a given sustained wind velocity. The U.S. Army Corps of Engineers (U.S. Army Coastal Engineering Research Center, 1984) devised the following equations for Airy waves (see Johnson, 1980):

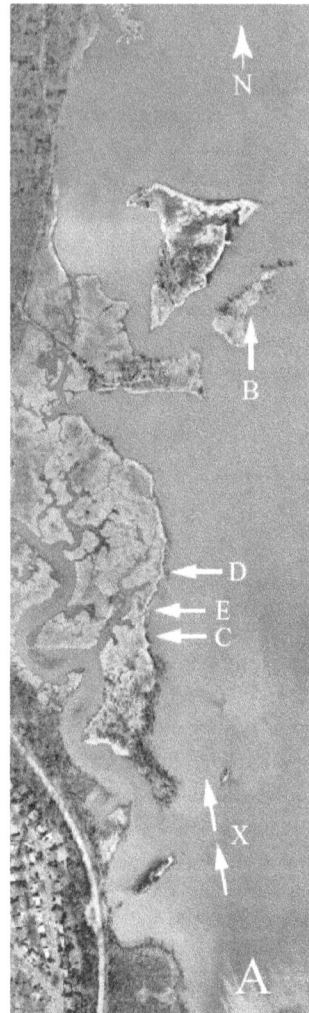

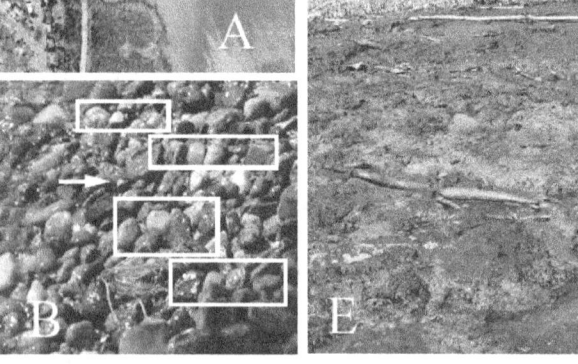

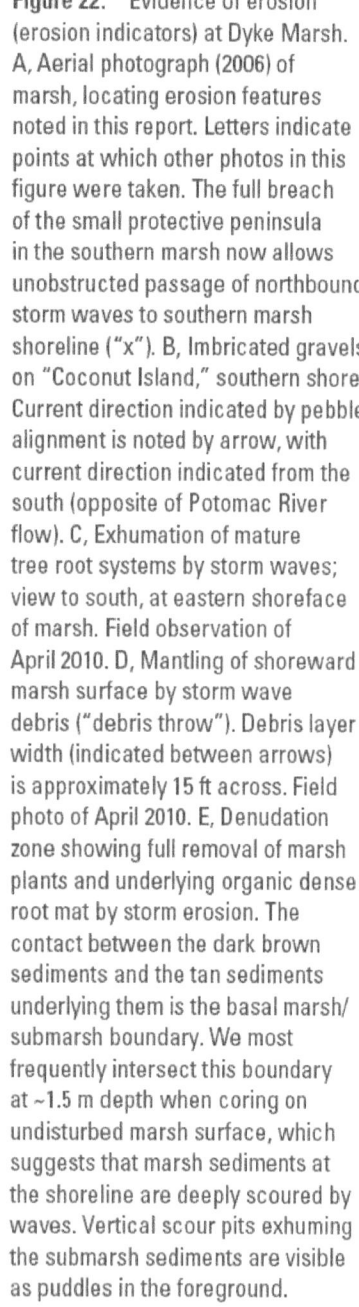

Figure 22. Evidence of erosion (erosion indicators) at Dyke Marsh. A, Aerial photograph (2006) of marsh, locating erosion features noted in this report. Letters indicate points at which other photos in this figure were taken. The full breach of the small protective peninsula in the southern marsh now allows unobstructed passage of northbound storm waves to southern marsh shoreline ("x"). B, Imbricated gravels on "Coconut Island," southern shore. Current direction indicated by pebble alignment is noted by arrow, with current direction indicated from the south (opposite of Potomac River flow). C, Exhumation of mature tree root systems by storm waves; view to south, at eastern shoreface of marsh. Field observation of April 2010. D, Mantling of shoreward marsh surface by storm wave debris ("debris throw"). Debris layer width (indicated between arrows) is approximately 15 ft across. Field photo of April 2010. E, Denudation zone showing full removal of marsh plants and underlying organic dense root mat by storm erosion. The contact between the dark brown sediments and the tan sediments underlying them is the basal marsh/submarsh boundary. We most frequently intersect this boundary at ~1.5 m depth when coring on undisturbed marsh surface, which suggests that marsh sediments at the shoreline are deeply scoured by waves. Vertical scour pits exhuming the submarsh sediments are visible as puddles in the foreground.

A   B

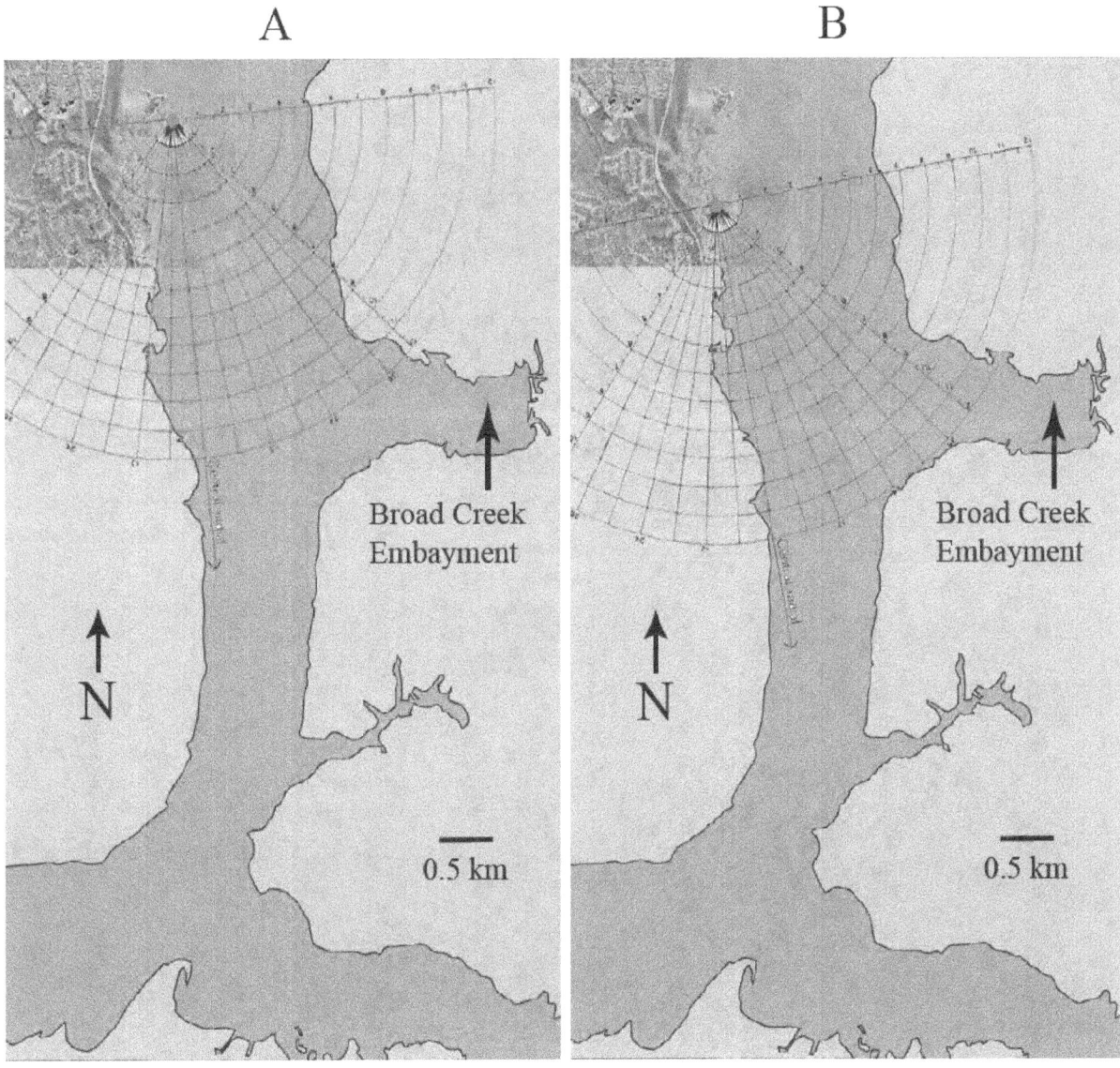

Figures 23A and 23B.   Aerial photographs of the Potomac River near Dyke Marsh with the fetch net oriented to maximum linear fetch. Red dot indicates the respective geographic point for which the fetch net equations were run. A–B, Photograph for 2002 and fetch net for the northern marsh (A) and the southern marsh (B). Scale bar at base of all photos is 0.5 km. The gray-tone portion of the base map for each figure was traced from 18 March 2006 orthoimagery found at *http://eros.usgs.gov* (see Appendix 3A, metadata for item #2).

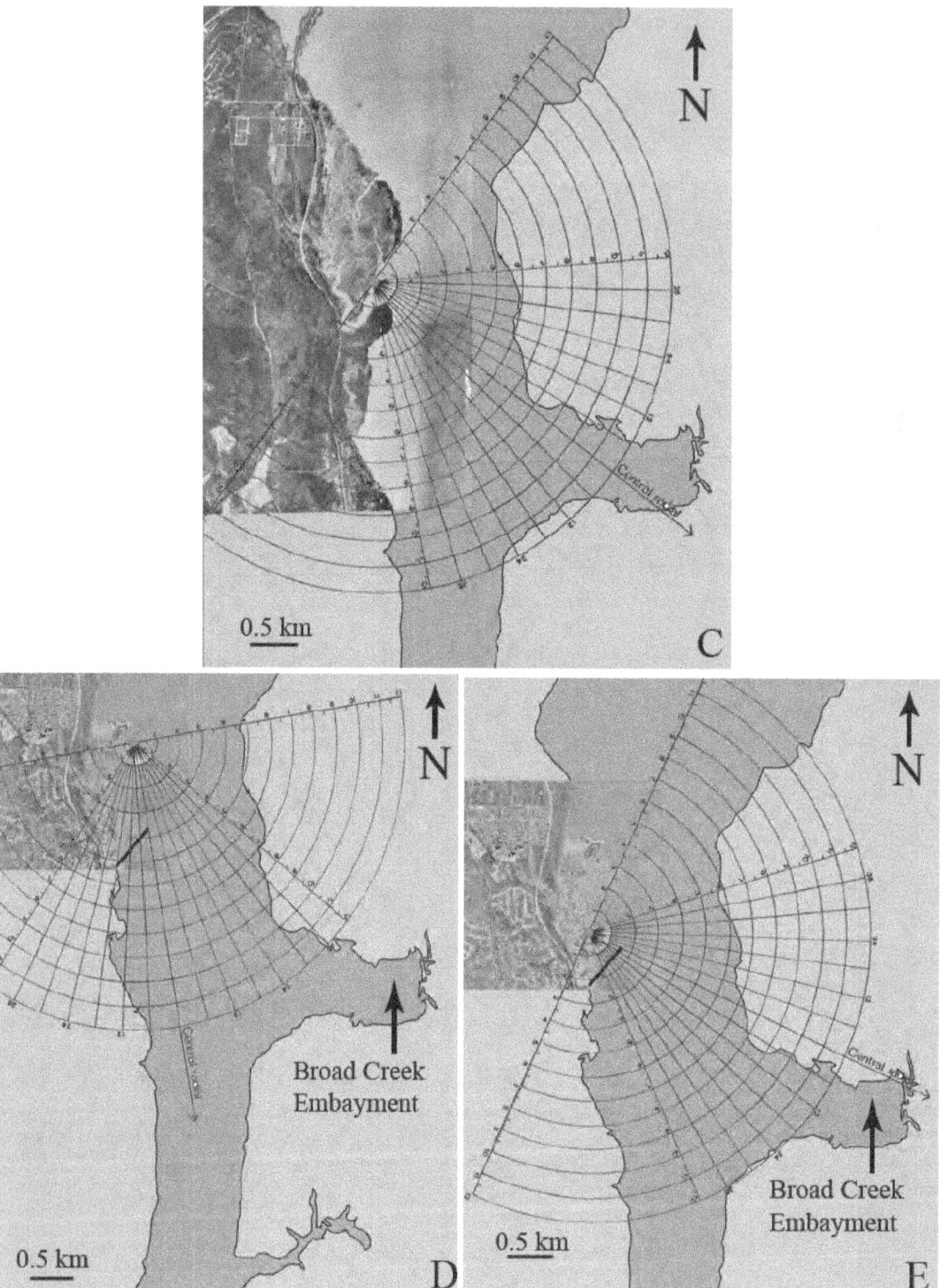

Figures 23C, 23D, and 23E.   Aerial photographs of the Potomac River near Dyke Marsh with the fetch net oriented to maximum linear fetch. Red dot indicates the respective geographic point for which the fetch net equations were run. C, Photograph for the 1937 marsh superimposed on a 2002 marsh background and the fetch net set for the southern portion. D–E, Photographs and localities are the same as for 23A and 23B, but a barrier (black bar) is placed in a similar orientation and length of the Hog Gut peninsula in the 1937 photo. The fetch orientation for E is the maximum for a southeastern wind source. Scale bar at base of all photos is 0.5 km. The gray-tone portion of the base map for each figure was traced from 18 March 2006 orthoimagery found at http://eros.usgs.gov (see Appendix 3A, metadata for item #2).

$$H = \left[\frac{w^2}{g}\right]\left[0.283 \cdot \tanh\left[0.53\left(\frac{gh}{w^2}\right)^{0.75}\right] \cdot \tanh\left[\frac{0.0125\left(\frac{gF}{w^2}\right)^{0.42}}{\tanh\left[0.53\left(\frac{gh}{w^2}\right)^{0.75}\right]}\right]\right] \qquad (2)$$

$$T = \left(\frac{2\pi w}{g}\right)\left[1.2 \cdot \tanh\left[0.833\left(\frac{gh}{w^2}\right)^{0.375}\right] \cdot \tanh\left[\frac{0.077\left(\frac{gF}{w^2}\right)^{0.25}}{\tanh\left[0.833\left(\frac{gh}{w^2}\right)^{0.375}\right]}\right]\right] \qquad (3)$$

where H is wave height and T is wave period. The wind speed is w, the water depth is h, and g is the gravitational constant. Once wave height and period are known, the wave length (L) can be determined iteratively from the equation:

$$L = \frac{gT^2}{2\pi} \cdot \tanh\left(\frac{2\pi h}{L}\right) \qquad (4)$$

The last part of the equation can be ignored for water depths where $2h > L$.

Once the wave height and wave length are determined, one can determine the bottom shear stress exerted by waves at a given depth. This is determined by the following relationships for orbital diameter (d_o) for the Airy wave:

$$d_o = \frac{H}{\sinh\left(\frac{2\pi h}{L}\right)} \qquad (5)$$

and the maximum horizontal velocity (u_m) at the base of the wave is provided by:

$$u_m = \frac{\pi d_o}{T} = \frac{\pi H}{T \sinh\left(\frac{2\pi h}{L}\right)} \qquad (6)$$

The relationship between this horizontal velocity and the largest sediment grain size (D) was experimentally derived by Komar and Miller (1973, 1975) and expressed by the equations:

$$\frac{\rho u_m^2}{(\rho_s - \rho)gD} = 0.46\pi\left(\frac{d_o}{D}\right)^{0.25} \text{ if } D > 0.5 \text{ mm} \qquad (7)$$

$$\frac{\rho u_m^2}{(\rho_s - \rho)gD} = 0.21\left(\frac{d_o}{D}\right)^{0.5} \text{ if } D < 0.5 \text{ mm} \qquad (8)$$

In these equations, ρ is the density of water and ρ_s is the density of a grain of sediment.

Where waves begin to shoal ($L > 20h$), the equations can be modified with the equations:

$$\frac{L}{L_\infty} = \left[\tanh\left(\frac{2\pi h}{L_\infty}\right)\right]^{0.5} \qquad (9)$$

$$\frac{H}{H_\infty} = \left(\frac{1}{2n}\frac{L_\infty}{L}\right)^{0.5} \qquad (10)$$

L_∞ and H_∞ are the deep water wave length and height and the ratio of wave group velocity to wave phase velocity (n) is given by the equation:

$$n = 0.5\left[1 + \frac{2kh}{\sinh(2kh)}\right] \qquad (11)$$

and k, which is the wave number, is given by the equation:

$$k = \frac{2\pi}{L_\infty} \qquad (12)$$

Rowan and others (1992) indicated a series of simplifications that are applicable as long as the water depth was greater than four times the wave length, the criterion for maintaining the Airy wave sinusoidal geometry. This geometry results in the wave length being approximately 20 times the wave height.

$$L = 20H \qquad (13)$$

Also, under these conditions, the maximum possible wave height (H_{max}) for a given effective fetch was determined by the U.S. Army Corps of Engineers (U.S. Army Coastal Engineering Research Center, 1984) to be

$$H_{max} = 0.332F^{0.5} \qquad (14)$$

These two simplifying equations allow one to express the wave length (L), period (T), and maximum horizontal velocity (u_m) for the largest possible deep-water wave at a given fetch and depth. The equations all expressed as functions of effective fetch are

$$L = 6.640F^{0.5} \qquad (15)$$

$$T = 2.061F^{0.25} \qquad (16)$$

$$u_m = \frac{0.506F^{0.25}}{\sinh\left(\frac{0.942h}{F^{0.5}}\right)} \qquad (17)$$

We solved these equations for five different scenarios (fig. 23, table 5). In the first case we examined the marsh configuration as of 2002 for the north end of the marsh near "Coconut Island" and the southern end of the marsh near "Angel Island." For comparison we also examined the southern marsh for 1937 (fig. 23C). We then solved for the first two localities, but with a barrier that extends to the former length of the Hog Island Gut peninsula (fig. 23D–E). We solved for the maximum deep-water Airy wave using the maximum effective fetch (equations 13–17) for all but the last scenario. In the case of the southern marsh with the barrier, the maximum fetch for the southeast was used. This is justified by the lack of erosional features from the northeast in the aerial photo record or ground observations, and by the fact that the marsh never was affected by northeastern erosion in the years prior to dredge mining, despite a similar northeastern fetch to the final scenario. We made corrections for changes in the wave properties due to shoaling to a depth of 1 m using equations 9–12. Finally, we ascertained the maximum grain sizes moved by these waves at that depth using equations 7 and 8, assuming a grain density of 2,650 kilograms per cubic meter (kg/m³) and water density of 1,000 kg/m³. We also used equations 2 to 6 to determine wave characteristics under conditions of sustained winds of 20 miles per hour (mph) (8.9408 meters per second) and 30 mph (13.4112 meters per second). These values and the maximum grain sizes moved by them were compared to those for the maximum wave model to check for discrepancies due to approximations.

In the 2002 configuration of Dyke Marsh, the maximum waves on the north end have a wave length of 11.3 m and a wave height of 56 cm, and on the south end have a wave

length of 10 m and a wave height of 50 cm. These waves are capable of moving pebbles 0.6 and 0.4 cm in diameter in 1 m of water, respectively. In comparison, the 1937 marsh had maximum potential waves with a wave length of 7.2 m and height of 36 cm, capable of moving granules 1.6 mm in diameter in 1 m of water. Furthermore, these maximum winds would have to have been generated from the east across the width of the river, rather than from the south along the river channel (fig. 23C). With the barrier in place, the maximum wave for the north marsh is reduced to 10.2 m wave length and 51 cm wave height, still capable of moving pebbles 0.5 cm in diameter in 1 m of water. The orientation of this maximum wave fetch, however, is decidedly more across the river than along the river axis (fig. 23D). In the southern marsh, the impact is more profound, with maximum wave length of 6.8 m and wave height of 34 cm, capable of moving granules 1.4 mm in diameter in 1 m of water. The maximum southeastern fetch in this scenario is almost directly across the river (fig. 23E). In all scenarios, the grain sizes moved by sustained 30-mph winds are similar to the maximum wave size values.

The photographic record and our observations on the marsh suggest that significant erosion is focused primarily on the southern or southeastern portions of the marsh. There is a moderate fetch to the northeast of Dyke Marsh, but no observable features reflecting waves generated from that direction. In the 1937 photo of Dyke Marsh, there is sufficient fetch to the northeast that a maximum wave capable of moving coarse sand could have affected the marsh, if the Broad Creek embayment to the southeast were included. The similarity of the 1864 map and 1937 photo again suggests that these orientations did not cause significant erosion. The lack of evidence of erosion from these directions may reflect random chance, or it may indicate that sufficient wind velocities are difficult to sustain in orientations other than along the river valley. We have insufficient data to rule out the potential for winds impacting Dyke Marsh from other directions or to constrain the potential for developing sustained wind velocities in any direction. Our models clearly indicate that even sustained winds at 20 mph are capable of moving coarse sand in 1 m of water in the current marsh configuration. In 1937, even maximum wave size could only move medium sand in the southern marsh, and the easternmost portion of the northern marsh was the only part exposed to potential waves similar to the modern maxima. If the peninsula were replaced today with no other modifications, the northern part of the marsh could still be impacted by waves capable of moving small pebbles. The waves, however, would have to be generated across the Broad Creek embayment. In the southern part of the marsh, only winds from the northeast would be able to generate waves capable of moving coarse sand, whereas waves from the south or southeast would only move very fine sand even with sustained winds of 30 mph. A more comprehensive assessment of potential wave effects would be obtained from calculating wave measurements on a grid, with multiple orientations for different wind velocities. Such an exercise is beyond the scope of this study.

Table 5. Equations used to determine maximum size of wind-driven waves and largest grain size moved for fetch conditions shown in figure 23

Row name	Fig. 23A	Fig. 23B	Fig. 23C	Fig. 23D	Fig. 23E	Values and functions
A	8.42	5.6	3.94	6.08	1.9	max fetch km
B	6.1	4.82	2.07	4.65	1.71	6 degree R
C	4.43	3.84	1.77	3.71	1.67	12 degree R
D	3.7	3.19	1.62	3.6	1.7	18 degree R
E	3.62	3.02	1.59	3.56	1.66	24 degree R
F	3.61	3.04	1.59	3.78	1.59	30 degree R
G	2.41	3.07	1.54	2.1	1.49	36 degree R
H	2.07	3.68	1.46	0.44	1.51	42 degree R
I	2.84	1.12	0.24	1.03	0.36	6 degree L
J	1.41	0.36	0.22	1.16	0.35	12 degree L
K	0.95	0.4	0.22	1.34	0.35	18 degree L
L	0.75	0.52	0.21	0.99	0.36	24 degree L
M	0.54	0.28	0.23	0.76	0.37	30 degree L
N	0.44	0.06	0.23	0.5	0.37	36 degree L
O	0.36	0.03	0.24	0.44	0.39	42 degree L
P	8.42	5.6	3.94	6.08	1.9	max fetch km
Q	6.0695	4.7959	2.05965	4.62675	1.70145	$B \times \cos 6$
R	4.33254	3.75552	1.73106	3.62838	1.63326	$C \times \cos 12$
S	3.5187	3.03369	1.54062	3.4236	1.6167	$D \times \cos 18$
T	3.30868	2.76028	1.45326	3.25384	1.51724	$E \times \cos 24$
U	3.12626	2.63264	1.37694	3.27348	1.37694	$F \times \cos 30$
V	1.94969	2.48363	1.24586	1.6989	1.20541	$G \times \cos 36$
W	1.53801	2.73424	1.08478	0.32692	1.12193	$H \times \cos 42$
X	2.8258	1.1144	0.2388	1.02485	0.3582	$I \times \cos 6$
Y	1.37898	0.35208	0.21516	1.13448	0.3423	$J \times \cos 12$
Z	0.90345	0.3804	0.20922	1.27434	0.33285	$K \times \cos 18$
A1	0.6855	0.47528	0.19194	0.90486	0.32904	$L \times \cos 24$
B1	0.46764	0.24248	0.19918	0.65816	0.32042	$M \times \cos 30$
C1	0.35596	0.04854	0.18607	0.4045	0.29933	$N \times \cos 36$
D1	0.26748	0.02229	0.17832	0.32692	0.28977	$O \times \cos 42$
E1	2.899866	2.254176	1.174138	2.373331852	1.062581	effective fetch km $(\sum P{-}D1)/13.5$
F1	2.826813	2.492309	1.798737	2.55733323	1.711154	Min depth $1.66 \times E1^{0.5}$
G1	0.565363	0.498462	0.359747	0.511466646	0.342231	Max H $0.332 \times E1^{0.5}$
H1	11.30725	9.969238	7.194947	10.22933292	6.844615	Max L $6.64 \times E1^{0.5}$
I1	2.689506	2.525369	2.145397	2.558100536	2.092515	Max T $2.061 \times E1^{0.25}$
J1	0.317699	0.298311	0.253426	0.30217688	0.247179	Max μ_m $0.56 \times E1^{0.25}/\sinh(0.946 \times F1/E1^{0.5})$
K1	1.570796	1.570796	1.570796	1.570796327	1.570796	$2\pi \times F1/H1$
L1	0.245671	0.2166	0.156324	0.222251288	0.148712	Max d_o $G1/\sinh K1$
M1	0.001124	0.00099	0.00072	0.001	0.00068	Grain size
N1	5.55336	5.558939	5.516457	5.646930546	5.556551	density side eq. 7 and 8 $1000 \times J1^2/(1650 \times 9.8 \times M1)$
O1	5.556542	5.557937	5.547288	5.579801846	5.55734	Right side eq. 7 $0.46\pi \times (L1/M1)^{0.25}$

Table 5. Equations used to determine maximum size of wind-driven waves and largest grain size moved for fetch conditions shown in figure 23.—Continued

Row name	Fig. 23A	Fig. 23B	Fig. 23C	Fig. 23D	Fig. 23E	Values and functions
P1	3.104654	3.106212	3.094321	3.130699893	3.105545	Right side eq. 8 $0.21 \times (L1/ M1)^{0.5}$
Q1	0.555678	0.630257	0.873277	0.614232165	0.917975	$2\pi/H1$
R1	0.504763	0.558229	0.703036	0.547099366	0.724938	$\tanh Q1$
S1	8.033428	7.448491	6.032763	7.566245334	5.827731	L for 1 m $H1 \times R1^{0.5}$
T1	0.555678	0.630257	0.873277	0.614232165	0.917975	Wave number $2\pi/H1$
U1	0.910191	0.888601	0.814104	0.893330373	0.800403	n in eq. 11 $0.5(1+2T1/\sinh(2T1))$
V1	0.497134	0.432574	0.307892	0.444917734	0.29314	H for 1 m $G1(1/2U1 \times H1/S1)^{0.5}$
W1	0.78213	0.843551	1.04151	0.830423153	1.078153	$2\pi/S1$
X1	0.671836	0.568116	0.363512	0.588026692	0.338669	μ_m for 1 m $\pi U1/(I1 \times \sinh W1)$
Y1	0.575156	0.45668	0.248243	0.478811724	0.225577	d_o for 1 m $G1/\sinh W1$
Z1	0.0063	0.0043	0.0016	0.0046	0.00137	Grain size
A2	4.430738	4.641904	5.107486	4.648643355	5.177513	density side eq. 7 and 8 $1000 \times X1^2/(1650 \times 9.8 \times Z1)$
B2	4.467032	4.639206	5.100313	4.615932405	5.176678	Right side eq. 7 $0.46\pi(Y1/ Z1)^{0.25}$
C2	2.006513	2.164169	2.615758	2.142509552	2.694674	Right side eq. 8 $0.21(Y1/ Z1)^{0.5}$
D2	0.693107	0.61109	0.441033	0.62703334	0.419558	$9.8 \times H1/2 \times (8.9408)^2$
E2	0.308048	0.271596	0.196015	0.278681484	0.18647	$9.8 \times H1/2 \times (13.4112)^2$
F2	355.5095	276.351	143.9436	290.9589919	130.2673	$9.8 \times E1 \times 1000/(8.9408)^2$
G2	158.0042	122.8227	63.97494	129.3151075	57.89656	$9.8 \times E1 \times 1000/(13.4112)^2$
H2	0.871566	0.831361	0.735659	0.839429036	0.722017	$D2^{0.375}$
I2	0.643031	0.613368	0.54276	0.619320625	0.532695	$E2^{0.375}$
J2	0.431656	0.414159	0.371273	0.41769564	0.365023	$\tanh(0.53 \times H2)$
K2	0.328197	0.314098	0.279982	0.316938391	0.275059	$\tanh(0.53 \times I2)$
L2	0.147322	0.132533	0.100775	0.135431398	0.096636	$0.125 \times (F2)^{0.42}$
M2	0.104797	0.094277	0.071686	0.096339127	0.068742	$0.125 \times (G2)^{0.42}$
N2	0.328633	0.309511	0.264954	0.313330877	0.258724	$\tanh J2/L2$
O2	0.308885	0.291452	0.250585	0.294939658	0.244842	$\tanh L2/M2$
P2	0.759627	0.691161	0.541194	0.704641106	0.521308	$D2^{0.75}$
Q2	0.413488	0.37622	0.294589	0.383558036	0.283764	$E2^{0.75}$
R2	0.486524	0.428092	0.302297	0.439584179	0.286115	H for 20 mph $8.162915 \times 0.283 \times \tanh(P2) \times N2$
S2	0.627983	0.544084	0.372695	0.560356864	0.351477	H for 30 mph $18.35309 \times 0.283 \times \tanh Q2 \times O2$
T2	0.620621	0.599601	0.546098	0.603887941	0.538073	$\tanh(0.833 \times H2)$
U2	0.489684	0.470674	0.42364	0.474524842	0.416736	$\tanh(0.833 \times I2)$
V2	0.334352	0.313947	0.26671	0.318015781	0.260135	$0.077 \times F2^{0.25}$
W2	0.272997	0.256336	0.217768	0.259658797	0.2124	$0.077 \times G2^{0.25}$
X2	2.10054	1.981702	1.70146	2.005509408	1.661908	T for 20 mph $5.732317 \times 1.2 \times T2 \times \tanh V2/T2$

Table 5. Equations used to determine maximum size of wind-driven waves and largest grain size moved for fetch conditions shown in figure 23.—Continued

Row name	Fig. 23A	Fig. 23B	Fig. 23C	Fig. 23D	Fig. 23E	Values and functions
Y2	2.557231	2.411123	2.06795	2.440362456	2.019651	T for 30 mph $8.598475 \times 1.2 \times U2 \times \tanh W2/U2$
Z2	6.881893	6.125238	4.515331	6.273293614	4.307848	L for 20 mph $9.8 \times X2^2/2\pi$
A3	10.19967	9.067442	6.670006	9.288698727	6.362077	L for 30 mph $9.8 \times Y2^2/2\pi$
B3	0.913002	1.025786	1.391522	1.001576794	1.458544	$2\pi/Z2$
C3	0.616019	0.692939	0.942006	0.676433319	0.9876	$2\pi/A3$
D3	0.72257	0.772213	0.883505	0.762255574	0.897369	$\tanh B3$
E3	0.54835	0.599867	0.736143	0.589195786	0.756337	$\tanh C3$
F3	5.849894	5.382592	4.244184	5.477040081	4.080807	L for 20 mph and 1m $Z2 \times D3^{0.5}$
G3	7.55292	7.022831	5.722782	7.129920595	5.532948	L for 30 mph and 1m $A3 \times E3^{0.5}$
H3	0.913002	1.025786	1.391522	1.001576794	1.458544	Wave number for 20 mph $2\pi Z2$
I3	0.616019	0.692939	0.942006	0.676433319	0.9876	Wave number for 30 mph $2\pi A3$
J3	0.80192	0.768124	0.672792	0.775253522	0.658251	n in eq. 11 for 20 mph $0.5(1+(2 \times H3/\sinh(2 \times H3)))$
K3	0.892805	0.869742	0.7931	0.874755191	0.779404	n in eq. 11 for 30 mph $0.5(1+(2 \times I3/\sinh(2 \times I3)))$
L3	0.416681	0.368445	0.268798	0.377815725	0.256204	H for 20 mph and 1m $R2 \times ((1/2 \times J3) \times (Z2/F3))^{0.5}$
M3	0.546122	0.468751	0.319472	0.483550154	0.301871	H for 30 mph and 1m $S2 \times ((1/2 \times K3) \times (A3/G3))^{0.5}$
N3	1.074068	1.167316	1.480422	1.147186293	1.539692	$2\pi F3$
O3	0.831888	0.89468	1.097925	0.881241975	1.135594	$2\pi G3$
P3	0.322303	0.253911	0.129005	0.266838781	0.115182	d_o for 20 mph $L3/\sinh N3$
Q3	0.586463	0.460053	0.23981	0.483640168	0.216256	d_o for 30 mph $M3/\sinh O3$
R3	0.48204	0.402525	0.238196	0.417997916	0.217734	μ_m for 20 mph $\pi P3/X2$
S3	0.720478	0.59943	0.364316	0.622612594	0.336389	μ_m for 30 mph $\pi Q3/Y2$
T3	0.00312	0.0021	0.000645	0.00227	0.000527	Grain size
U3	4.605764	4.77152	5.439999	4.760059215	5.563279	density side eq. 7 and 8 20 mph $1000 \times R3^2/(1650 \times 9.8 \times T3)$
V3	4.607179	4.792071	5.434622	4.758427721	5.556493	Right side eq. 7 20 mph $0.46\pi(P3/T3)^{0.25}$
W3	2.134391	2.309141	2.969905	2.27683123	3.104599	Right side eq. 8 20 mph $0.21(P3/T3)^{0.5}$
X3	0.00745	0.00495	0.00164	0.0054	0.001365	Grain size
Y3	4.308989	4.489121	5.004971	4.439479176	5.126739	density side eq. 7 and 8 30 mph $1000 \times S3^2/(1650 \times 9.8 \times X3)$
Z3	4.304561	4.487023	5.02532	4.445696955	5.127039	Right side eq. 7 30 mph $0.46\pi(Q3/X3)^{0.25}$
A4	1.863209	2.024513	2.539401	1.987392272	2.643244	Right side eq. 8 30 mph $0.21(Q3/X3)^{0.5}$

Frequency of Potentially Damaging Storms at Dyke Marsh (1937–2009)

The geologic indicators of erosion that we observed in the field and the wave-fetch solutions discussed above suggest that the marsh shoreline has been especially susceptible to erosion when the sustained winds are strong (>20 mph) and blowing toward the north or northwest. Winter storms (nor'easters) can deliver these wind-field conditions and can induce strong shoreline erosion (Dolan and Davis, 1992; Goodbred and Hine, 1995; Kocin and others, 1995; Cardone and others, 1996), but we only used more readily available summer storm data to calculate a minimum recurrence frequency estimate of damaging storms at Dyke Marsh (appendix 4). Conversely, these data can also be used to estimate the maximum lull frequency between such storms. We are still acquiring winter storm data for similar analysis.

We compiled National Oceanic and Atmospheric Administration (NOAA) website data to analyze the storm tracks of the 760 Atlantic tropical depressions occurring between 1937 and 2009 (source: NOAA Coastal Services Center, http://cscs-maps-q.csc.noaa.gov/hurricanes/viewer.html). Of these, we identified those tropical depressions, tropical storms, and hurricanes that crossed into Virginia or in close enough proximity to Dyke Marsh to deliver such winds.[11] The storm tracks of these 43 potential erosion events are illustrated in appendix 4. Of those, 24 actually were tropical storms or hurricanes (sustained winds ≥ 39 mph and ≥ 74 mph, respectively).

Figure 24A illustrates the frequency of tropical depression activity in the Atlantic from 1937 to 2009 (top of figure, scale along left axis). The base of this same graph plots the frequency of all tropical depressions, tropical storms, and hurricanes that potentially affected Dyke Marsh (scale along right axis). We observed that the Atlantic Ocean showed increased storm activity from 1945 to 1955 and from 1995 to 2005. There is a concurrent modest rise in the number of storms that tracked toward Dyke Marsh during those Atlantic storm activity maxima, but the correlation is not strong. The highest number of tropical depressions, tropical storms, and hurricanes that tracked near Dyke Marsh in a given year occurred in 2004, which included the storm remnants of Hurricanes Charley, Gaston, Ivan, and Jeanne.

Figure 24B illustrates the same tropical depression activity in the Atlantic (top of figure, scale along left axis), while the base of that same graph plots the frequency only of those tropical storms and hurricanes that potentially affected Dyke Marsh—storms with sustained winds of 39 mph or greater. Again, we observed there were slight increases in target storms near Dyke Marsh that coincided with overall increases in Atlantic storm activity.

These data indicate that tropical depressions, tropical storms, and hurricanes approached or crossed over Dyke Marsh moderately often between 1937 and 2009. This finding is consistent with our observation that almost annual erosional

---

[11] Because winds in tropical storms and nor'easters are cyclonic (rotate counterclockwise) it is the northern edge of such storms that delivers damaging winds northward to northwestward against the marsh.

Atlantic tropical depression activity vs. tropical depression, tropical storm and hurricane tracks likely affecting Dyke Marsh

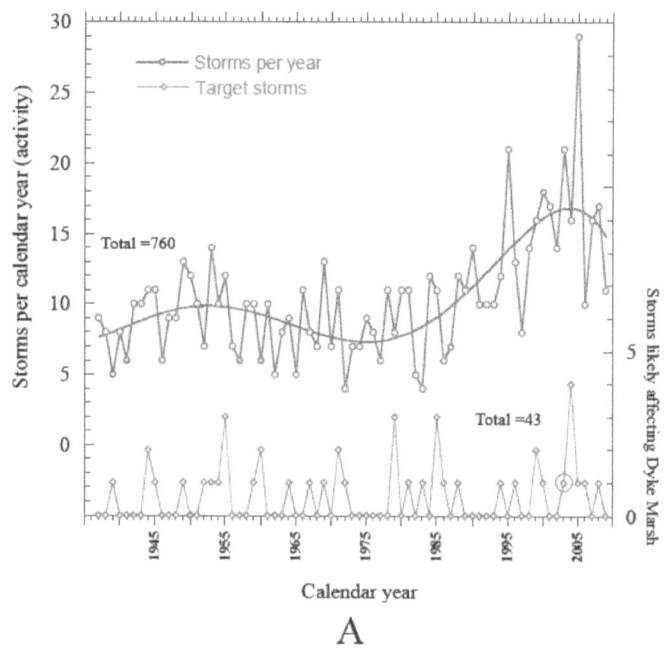

A

Atlantic tropical depression activity vs. tropical storm and hurricane tracks likely affecting Dyke Marsh

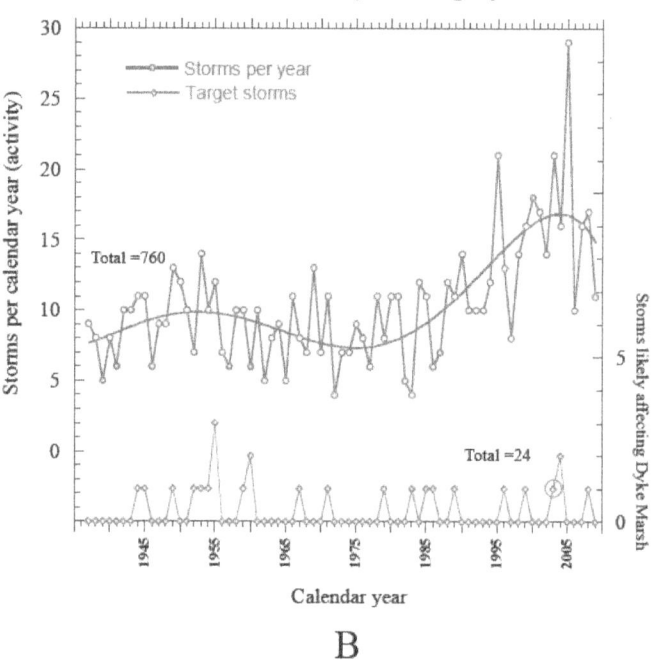

B

Figure 24. A, Atlantic tropical depression activity versus tropical depression, tropical storm, and hurricane tracks likely affecting Dyke Marsh. Data from 1937 to 2009; source: NOAA. The Hurricane Isabel event is circled in red. B, Atlantic tropical depression activity versus tropical storm and hurricane tracks likely affecting Dyke Marsh. Data from 1937 to 2009; source: NOAA. Tropical storms and hurricanes produce sustained winds of 39+ mph, above the fetch threshold for damaging storm waves at the marsh.

changes in the marsh profile were visible in our aerial photograph dataset from 1987 to 2002. Figure 24A plots 43 such occurrences in a 72-year period, for an average recurrence of 1 event per 1.67 years of weather record. Figure 24B plots 24 of the stronger events during the same time period, indicating an average recurrence of 1 event per 3.0 years. We used these data to calculate quiescent intervals as well, to derive initial estimates for historical quiet periods when potentially destructive summer storms likely did not visit Dyke Marsh.

Figure 25A plots the frequency of historic quiet intervals between all potentially damaging storms (summer only, including all nearby tropical depressions, tropical storms, and hurricanes). Approximately 90 percent of all the quiet historic intervals were 3 years or less in duration, although lulls in tropical events (in the broad sense) extended to as much as 6 consecutive calendar years. Figure 25B plots the frequency of storm lulls only for the more significant events (winds >39 mph, tropical storms and hurricanes). Approximately 75 percent of these quiet periods also were 3 years or less in duration, with a maximum observed value of 9 years. This value range (<1 to 3 years) represents the most frequently occurring maximum interval between potentially damaging storms, whether the lesser strength tropical depressions were included or not. By definition it represents the maximum duration between storms and not a minimum duration, because it presently excludes all winter storm data. Once we acquire and analyze the winter storm track data (nor'easters) through this same period of weather record, we predict that the maximum and average durations of the observed quiet periods between destructive storms at Dyke Marsh likely will diminish.

Continuous Versus Discontinuous (Episodic) Erosion Events

Evidence indicates that both continuous and episodic erosion now occurs at Dyke Marsh. A continuous, low-level removal of the marsh's organic mat by waves during high tide and low tide was observed during our 2009–2010 fieldwork (fig. 26), particularly in areas where the marsh had been disrupted previously by storm action. This erosion appears to be persistent but relatively low grade in its effect and is not quantified in this report. Aerial photographs and field evidence suggest that episodic, large-scale erosion events may have had greater collective impact on the deconstruction of the marsh. A primary example of such an event was Hurricane Isabel of September 18–19, 2003. It was the strongest tropical storm track we have identified that approached Dyke Marsh between 1937 and 2009 (event circled in red in fig. 24).

Photo evidence suggests that Hurricane Isabel (2003; cover photo; appendix 3) probably was responsible for a substantial amount of shoreline erosion to the marsh. Aerial photos taken during 2002 (before) and 2006 (after) of Dyke Marsh show visible differences in the eastern face of the southern marsh (fig. 27). We think it likely that the greatest amount of destruction to the marsh woodland (exhumed tree

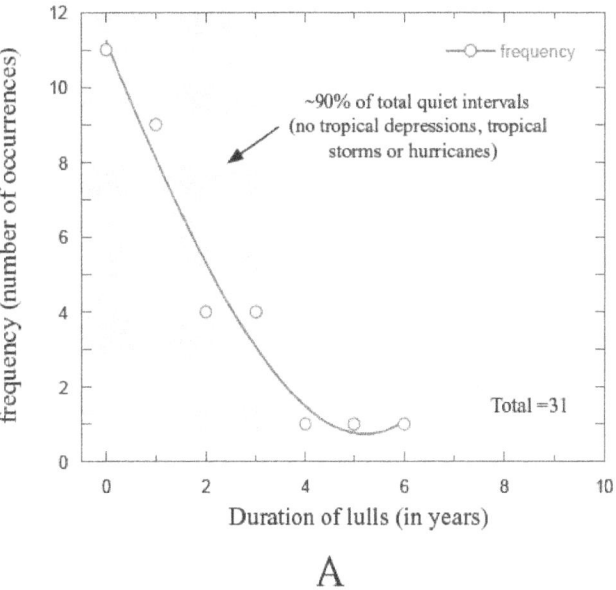

Lulls between consecutive tropical depressions, tropical storms, and hurricanes near Dyke Marsh (1937-2009)

A

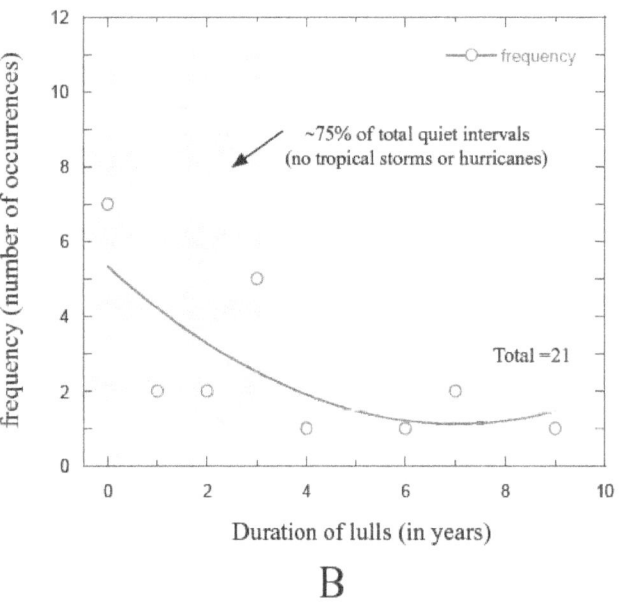

Lulls between consecutive tropical storms and hurricanes near Dyke Marsh (1937-2009)

B

Figure 25. Frequency of non-storm intervals (lull frequency) at Dyke Marsh. A, Lulls between consecutive tropical depressions, tropical storms, and hurricanes near Dyke Marsh (1937–2009). Data source: NOAA. B, Lulls between consecutive tropical storms and hurricanes near Dyke Marsh (1937–2009). Data source: NOAA. Note that both graphs (A and B) suggest that ≥75 percent of all likely storm lulls at Dyke Marsh were <1 to 3 years in length, suggesting that tropical storms are a regular occurrence at the marsh.

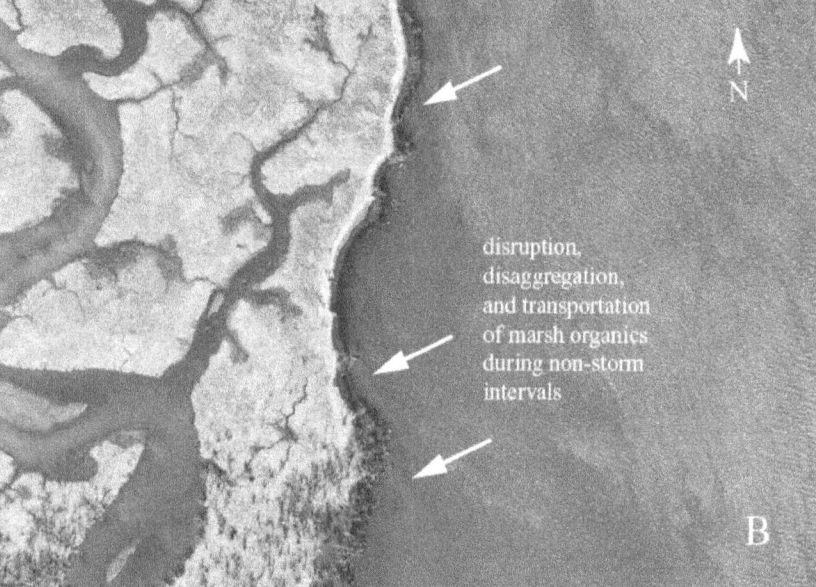

Figure 26. Non-storm conditions showing calm-weather wave disruption, re-suspension, and removal of the organic root mat underlying the marsh, during both high tide (A) and low tide (B). A, Non-storm disintegration of marsh's organic mat by wave action at high tide. Field photo April 2010. B, Aerial imagery showing wave erosion and stripping of marsh organic layer during non-storm low tide.

root systems and in situ toppled trees in the southern marsh) may be attributable to this single storm. However, we do not yet have all of the time-correlative winter storm data that would confirm or exclude them as co-contributors to this extensive erosion event. In particular, the winter storm of February 12, 2006 ("Blizzard of 2006," appendix 5), also may have been partly responsible for the strong erosion sustained by the marsh during this time interval.

Other hurricanes that tracked northeastward along the coast but did not make landfall near Virginia during this interval were not included as "potential event storms" in this report. However, those still may have triggered erosion events at Dyke Marsh. We omitted them in our counts in order to provide the most conservative estimate of the number of potentially damaging storms to visit the marsh. Examples of such peripheral storms include Hurricane Gladys (1968), Hurricane Gerda (1969), and Tropical Storm Gabrielle (2007; appendix 3).

Climate Change and Relative Sea-Level Rise Versus Dyke Marsh Aggradation

Relative sea-level rise is an additional factor to be considered regarding the marsh's potential sustainability. Our initial results suggest that ~3.06 to 5.25 mm/yr of compacted sediment has been accumulating on the marsh over the past half millennium. Our research on this topic is ongoing. Currently we are collecting and analyzing data across the marsh to determine long term aggradation values and patterns. Several published estimates for relative sea-level rise in the Chesapeake Bay area suggest rates of ~3.3 mm/yr (Donoghue, 1990) and ~3.1 mm/yr (Engelhart and others, 2009). These rates are similar to but less than our average of four preliminary sedimentation rates we derived For Dyke Marsh (~4.5 mm/yr, average of non-reworked samples from table 1), suggesting that sedimentation at the marsh potentially could be sufficient to compensate for relative sea-level rise at the marsh site. However, more conclusive evidence regarding marsh accumulation rates and relative sea-level rise will be available once our present coring transect is completed and our data are fully collected and analyzed.

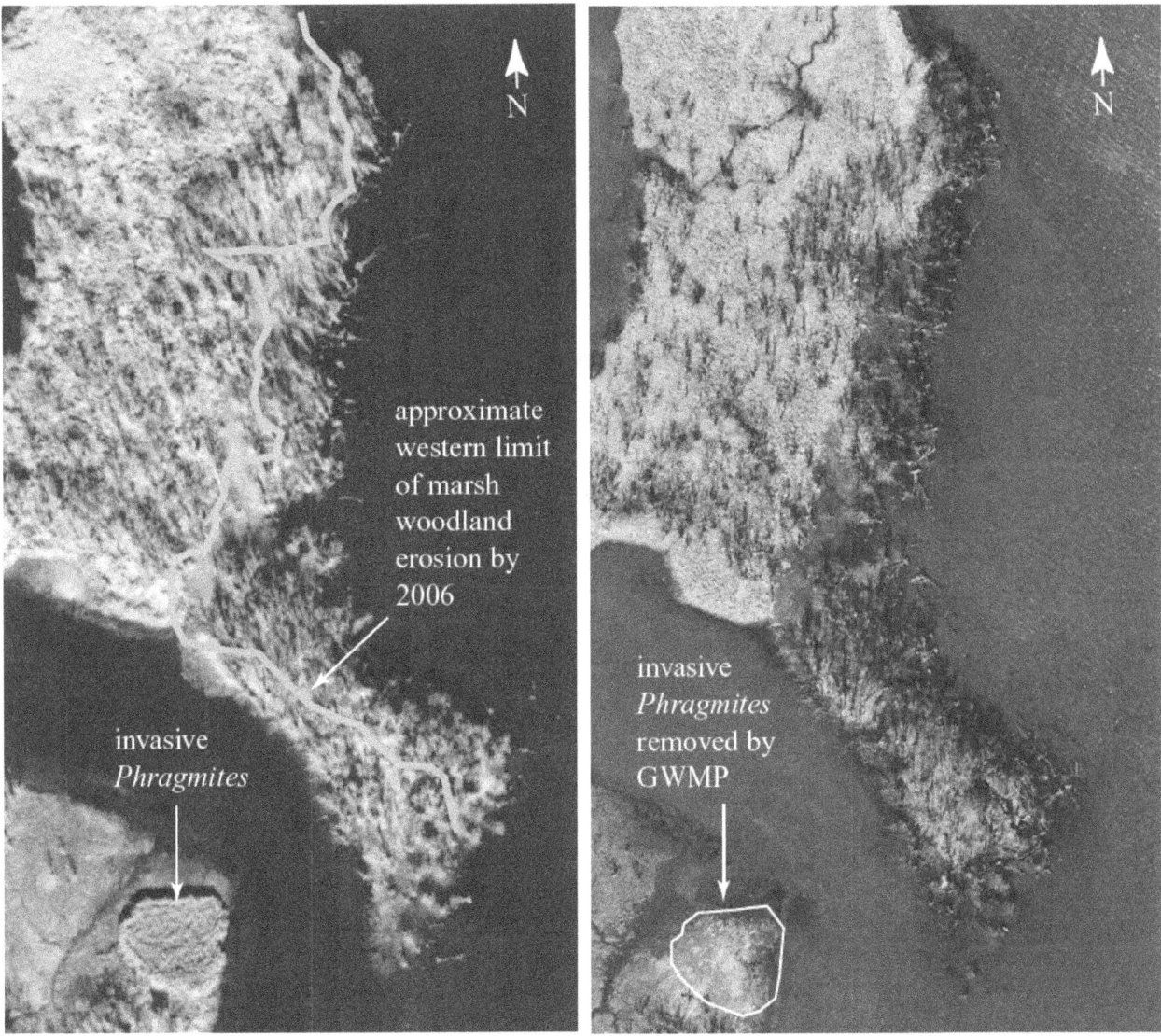

A, Southern part of marsh woodland in 2002   B, Southern part of marsh woodland in 2006

Figure 27. Comparison of two aerial photographs of the southern marsh woodland, showing strong forest erosion, likely from the storm waves generated by Hurricane Isabel (2003). A, Before, 2002. B, After, 2006.

Synthesis

Estimation of Marsh's Potential Sustainability

A number of geologic factors currently are operating independently, but with collective effect, to complicate the marsh's ability to sustain itself naturally. The weight of geologic evidence suggests that the shoreline along the southern marsh is now one of the most vulnerable areas of the marsh, for the following reasons. First, it remains exposed to shoreline erosion that appears to occur most frequently during tropical (summer) storms and nor'easter (winter) storms. Analysis of the summer half of that total dataset (the "warm-cored"

storms) reveals that the most frequent lull interval between consecutive potentially destructive storms is <1 to 3 years. Second, continuous mining of the marsh from ~1940 to 1972 removed much of its original extent (~101 acres). The northern marsh now consists only of several small eroding islands and an artificially extended peninsula (Haul Road) comprised largely of construction fill that was in place by the early 1970s. This backfill substrate differs in its material characteristics from those of the original marsh sediments, and consequently it does not support growth of the original marsh vegetation community in the same way. Rather, it now supports invasive, non-native plant growth that in several places is outcompeting native plant species in the marsh. The northern islands are relatively small marsh remnants, and eroding, but apparently not at the rate of the southern marsh's erosion. Third, dredge mining has deconstructed three of the four significant tidal channel networks that originally spanned the marsh and delivered sediment across its pre-mining (1937) configuration. Creation of deep mining scars parallel to the marsh shoreline, on the site where originally there was healthy marsh, contributes to the aggressive lateral erosion of HIG, the sole remaining tidal channel network in Dyke Marsh. Fourth, mining out the original southern shoreline of HIG (that is, the promontory that originally formed the northern end of Hog Island) has removed wave protection of the south marsh that existed historically back to at least 1864. Fifth, the removal of the promontory also has reconfigured the outflow of HIG such that it now is being siphoned during tidal ebb stage on the Potomac (its outflow is now subparallel to the main Potomac River flow). Bathymetric evidence (fig. 11) and aerial photos combine to suggest that HIG is eroding laterally and deepening. Consequently, HIG appears to be transforming from a depositional tidal creek network into an erosional one, at least since 1992. These human-induced and natural factors create a significant collective threat to the ability of the marsh to sustain itself under the current setting.

An estimate of those specific areas that pose relatively greater or lesser risk to Dyke Marsh's sustainability is illustrated in figure 28. This figure is a first-order risk assessment map, derived from our field observations, the bathymetric surveys of 1992 and 2009, aerial photographs, and the summary report by Normandeau Associates (2009). White areas represent emergent marsh, marsh woodland, forested floodplain, and reclaimed land. Green areas represent previously mined locations that are underwater, but areas specifically that have accumulated sediment between 1992 and 2009. These are areas of relatively lesser risk to the sustainability of the marsh. Red areas also represent previously mined locations that now are underwater, but those areas that conversely are still actively eroding (1992 to 2009). These red areas are eroding partly as a result of the scour channels (former mine scars) incised across this area, channels which now are increasing in width and depth. Red areas pose greater risk to the marsh's long term survival than green areas. Purple areas are locations that formerly were emergent land in 1992 but which have been eroded away by storm activity by 2009. The boundary between the white and purple represents those areas of marsh

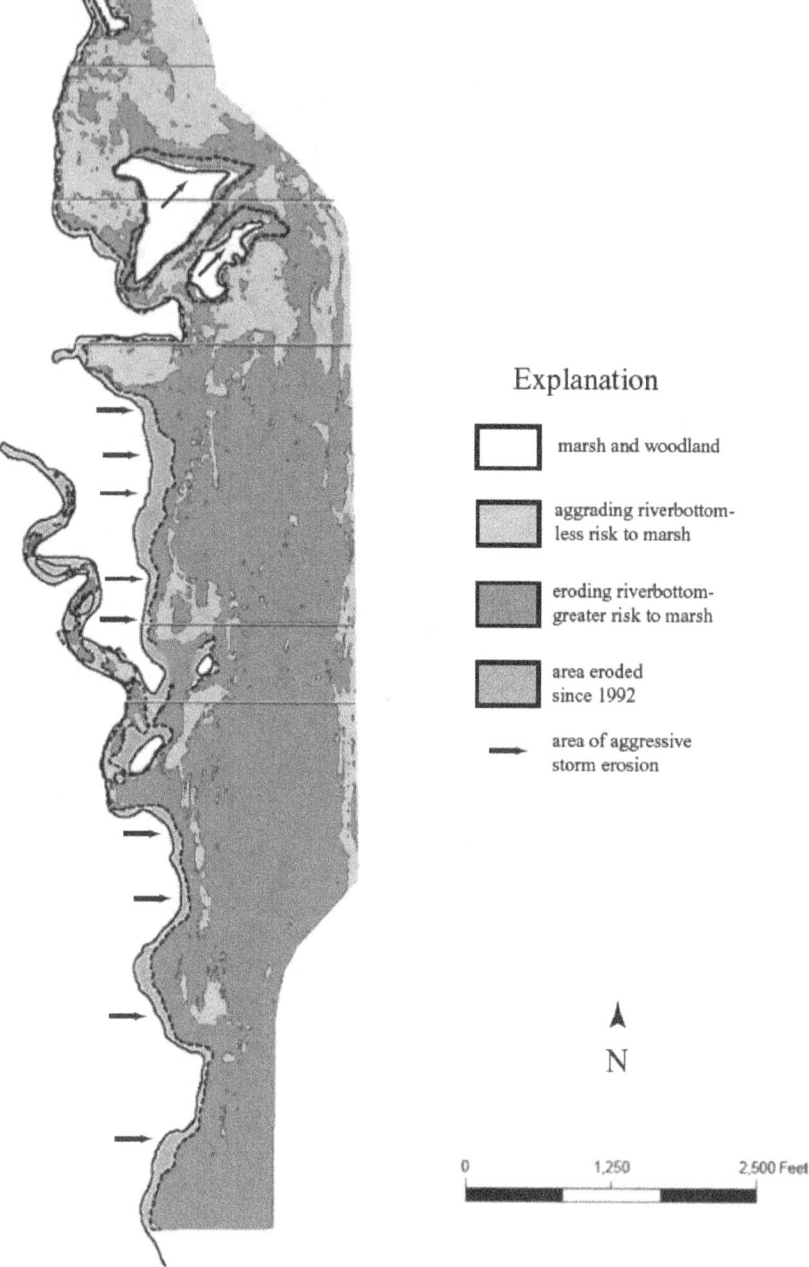

Figure 28. Preliminary risk assessment map for the sustainability of Dyke Marsh, based on the bathymetry synthesis (fig. 11), aerial photographs from 1987 to 2006, and field observations on the marsh (this report).

shoreline that now are being eroded aggressively by storms (arrows). Relatively more erosional features are located in the southern end of the marsh.

Geomorphic (Topographic) Changes Favoring Sedimentation and Marsh Stability

Erosion-related features dominate the field evidence we observed at Dyke Marsh: (1) toppled forests, (2) denuded, scoured, and debris-mantled marsh, (3) gravel beds that exhibit imbrication perpendicular to river current, and (4) tidal tributary piracy and historic foreshortening of the effective mouth of the last remaining significant tidal channel network in Dyke Marsh. Although the marsh has deposited sediment vertically at a rate between 3.06 and 5.25 mm/yr, its shoreline is now being stripped of sediment laterally at a rate between 6 and 7.8 ft/yr (~1,829 and ~2,377 mm/yr). The significant divergence between the vertical deposition rates and the lateral erosion rates emphasizes that the marsh presently is in a disequilibrium state and likely cannot sustain itself under present conditions.

Any medium- to long-term mitigation efforts put in place for restoring the marsh might be more effective if they first address this imbalance. Several protections can be restored that will diminish persistent geologic degradation of Dyke Marsh. One of these threats is posed by the extended wave fetch distance and late-stage shoaling in wave travel path against the marsh (that is, the ability of storm waves to penetrate across the shallow western Potomac River bottom directly to the eastern marsh face, using the two deep offshore scar channels that were cut into the shallow river bottom post-1937). Another threat is posed by the shortening and reorientation of HIG. Restoration of part of its lost channel length and reorientation back to its initial northeast outflow orientation are probable mandatory prerequisites for restoring it back to a dominantly aggradational tidal creek system; it is possible a well-designed wave break could accomplish this. However, designing a manmade wave break that would diminish wave erosion and redirect, protect, and lengthen the effective tidal network of HIG is beyond the scope of this project. That stipulated, such a design might best emulate the natural geologic protections provided by the formerly existing promontory at the southern end of HIG from 1864 to 1937. That original promontory helped to buffer wave fetch, directed the outflow of HIG northeastward against dominant Potomac River flow, and appears to have been low enough to be breachable by high-stage flooding on the Potomac. This latter characteristic may be important for preventing excessive funneling of Potomac floodwater up the mouth of HIG, toward the George Washington Parkway. Removal of these main environmental stressors—by re-introducing natural protections—would help to shift net geologic processes on the marsh away from wave-induced lateral degradation and internal erosion and back to a more sheltered aggradation and marsh building. This is the same way the marsh developed initially—through suspended sediment brought in by daily tides and trapped by submersed aquatic vegetation. Restoration of protections would favor increased sedimentation not only on the marsh proper but also in its nearshore environment, where marsh previously existed historically at Dyke Marsh. This natural deposition would be most stable long term if the deep bifurcated channel now paralleling the eastern shoreline were rendered nonfunctional. Impeding or terminating the existing function of this incised bifurcated river-bottom channel as a secondary erosional thalweg (that is, restoring it to a shallow river bottom that slopes eastward) would be a key factor in restoring long-term depositional equilibrium to the marsh.

Conclusions

Our field observations, laboratory analyses, and photographic analyses lead us to conclude the following. Dyke Marsh is a naturally occurring freshwater marsh that has existed on the western shore of the Potomac River since at least the 15th century. Historic maps and photographs suggest that the marsh appeared to be stable depositionally from about 1864 to 1937. The existence of accurate mapping of the marsh's configuration prior to 1864 remains unconfirmed. Mining of the marsh removed its depositional stability and consumed a significant portion of this wetland, ~ 90 to 101 acres, excluding the dredging on Hog Island. Removal by mining of a promontory on the southern periphery of the marsh also removed historic geological protections to the marsh and altered the size and function of its remaining significant tidal creek network. Dredging of the marsh also likely created the long bifurcated riverbed scar parallel to its present shoreline. Bathymetric data now indicate this scar has become an eroding secondary river channel, as marsh existed on that site prior to mining. Previously, only shallow, stable, gently sloping river bottom existed adjacent to the marsh's eastern shoreface, on the basis of bathymetry data from 1864, 1906, and 1931. These collective physiographic changes have altered the geologic setting of the marsh, and as a consequence the marsh is now subject to significant lateral erosion by storm waves, especially those generated by winds traveling upriver. This erosion has been dismantling the southern marsh and marsh woodland laterally since 1959. This erosion also is breaching and deconstructing the Hog Island Gut tidal creek network.

On the basis of the NOAA data we compiled, it appears that damaging storms have the potential to occur at Dyke Marsh with moderate frequency. Our analysis of archived NOAA data suggests that tropical storms and hurricanes probably affect Dyke Marsh approximately every 3.0 years on average. However, both summer storms and winter storms are capable of eroding the marsh shoreline. We analyzed only the summer storm frequency in this report. The longest quiet period between such storms that we observed was 6 to 9 years; most frequently these lull periods averaged <1 to 3 years between storms.

Given the suggested frequency of the storms (probably even higher, given that winter storm data are excluded here) and the nature of the present erosion at the marsh, we conclude that the marsh is not in a geologically stable state. The marsh will continue to be subjected to strong lateral shoreline erosion and stream piracy until its former geological protections are restored, or until it is fully dismembered by repeated storm activity. The minimal primary protections that likely are needed to protect and enhance natural deposition at the marsh include a functional wave break at the position of the former promontory and an effective blockage of the deep scar channels that parallel the shoreline within the Dyke Marsh eastern boundary.

Acknowledgments

We acknowledge with gratitude the Superintendent of the GWMP and Dyke Marsh, Dottie Marshall (NPS). Her support for this research, logistical and otherwise, has been exemplary. The bulk of this study has been funded by the Quaternary Landscape Response to Climate Change Project (to M.J. Pavich), USGS Climate Change Program. We thank David Bornholdt (USGS) and the National Research Program (NRP) for funding a part of this study. Similarly, we thank Diane Pavek (NPS, National Capital Region), James L. Sherald (former Director, Center for Urban Ecology), and Dan Sealy (Acting Director, Center for Urban Ecology) for their institutional support and insight during this study. We are indebted to Daffny Hoskie, Deborah Melvin, and Steve Boska (USFWS, Elizabeth Hartwell Mason Neck National Wildlife Refuge) for sharing their data and insight on the cliff-face loss at the Great Blue Heron rookery at Mason Neck. Our exceptional thanks to Robert Blama, U.S. Army Corps of Engineers, who originally contracted many of the aerial photographs of Dyke Marsh (especially the 1987 to 2002 imagery) that made our shoreline loss analyses possible. Likewise we are indebted to Cynthia Wanschura (NPS), Tammy Stidham (NPS), Diane Eldridge (USGS), Kevin Foley (USGS), Dave Weary (USGS), Randy Orndorff (USGS), Vanessa Kubick (NPS), and Zachary Glenn (NPS), who led us to suitable recent public domain aerial imagery of Dyke Marsh. We thank L. Scott Eaton, Geology Department, James Madison University, for material support (range-finding equipment and helpful discussions) regarding this study. Finally, we thank John Repetski and Kevin Foley (USGS) for insightful reviews of this manuscript, and Kathie Rankin and John Watson (USGS) for exceptional editing of the final report. This study was made possible only through the help of those listed above, and we are deeply grateful for their assistance.

References Cited

Barrows, E.M., Arsenault, S.B., and Grenier, N.P., 2008, Firefly (Coleoptera: Lampyridae) flight periods, sex ratios, and habitat frequencies in a United States Mid-Atlantic freshwater tidal marsh, low forest, and their ecotone: Banisteria, v. 31, p. 47–52.

Barrows, E.M., and Flint, O.S., Jr., 2009, Mecopteran (Mecoptera: Bittacidae, Meropeidae, Panorpidae) flight periods, sex ratios, and habitat frequencies in a United States Mid-Atlantic freshwater tidal marsh, low forest, and their ecotone: Journal of the Kansas Entomological Society, v. 82, no. 3, p. 223–230.

Barrows, E.M., McIntyre, A.M., and Flint, O.S., Jr., 2004, Alderfly (Neuroptera: Sialidae) flight periods, sex ratios, and habitat use in a Virginia freshwater tidal marsh, low forest, and their ecotones: Proceedings of the Washington Entomological Society, v. 107, p. 693–699.

Cardone, V.J., Jensen, R.E., Resio, D.T., Swail, V.R., and Cox, A.T., 1996, Evaluation of contemporary ocean wave models in rare extreme events—The "Halloween storm" of October 1991 and the "Storm of the century" of March 1993: Journal of Atmospheric and Oceanic Technology, v. 13, p. 198–230.

Carter, V., and Rybicki, N., 1986, Resurgence of submersed aquatic macrophytes in the tidal Potomac River, Maryland, Virginia, and the District of Columbia: Estuaries, v. 9, no. 4B, p. 366–375.

Carter, V., Rybicki, N.B., Anderson, R.T., Trombley, T.J., and Zynjuk, G.L., 1985, Data on the distribution and abundance of submersed aquatic vegetation in the tidal Potomac River and transition zone of the Potomac estuary, Maryland, Virginia, and the District of Columbia, 1983–1984: U.S. Geological Survey Open-File Report 85–82, 61 p.

Carter, V., Rybicki, N.B., Landwehr, J.M., and Tutora, M., 1994, Role of weather and water quality in population dynamics of submersed macrophytes in the tidal Potomac River: Estuaries, v. 17, no. 2, p. 417–426.

Crowley, T.J., 2000, Causes of climate change over the past 1000 years: Science, v. 289, p. 270–277.

Dolan, R., and Davis, R.E., 1992, An intensity scale for Atlantic Coast northeast storms: Journal of Coastal Research, v. 8, no. 4, p. 840–853.

Donoghue, J.F., 1990, Trends in Chesapeake Bay sedimentation rates during the late Holocene: Quaternary Research, v. 34, no. 1, p. 33–46.

Engelhardt, K.A.M., 2006, Relating effect and response traits in submersed aquatic macrophytes: Ecological Applications, v. 16, p. 1808–1820.

Engelhart, S.E., Horton, B.P., Douglas, B.C., Peltier, W.R., and Tornqvist, T.E., 2009, Spatial variability of late Holocene and 20th century sea-level rise along the Atlantic Coast of the United States: Geology, v. 37, p. 1115–1118.

Goodbred, S.L., Jr., and Hine, A.C., 1995, Coastal storm deposition—Salt-marsh response to a severe extratropical storm, March 1993, west-central Florida: Geology, v. 23, p. 679–682.

Hakanson, L., and Jansson, M., 1983, Principles of Lake Sedimentology: New York, Springer-Verlag, 316 p.

Hopfensperger, K.N., and Engelhardt, K.A.M., 2007, Coexistence of *Typha angustifolia* and *Impatiens capensis* in a tidal freshwater marsh: Wetlands, v. 27, no. 3, p. 561–569.

Hopfensperger, K.N., and Engelhardt, K.A.M., 2008, Annual species abundance in a freshwater tidal marsh—Germination and survival across an elevational gradient: Wetlands, v. 28, p. 521–526.

Hopfensperger, K.N., Engelhardt, K.A.M., and Seagle, S.W., 2007, Ecological feasibility studies in restoration decisionmaking: Environmental Management, v. 39, p. 843–852.

Hopfensperger, K.N., Kaushal, S.S., Findlay, S.E.G., and Cornwell, J.C., 2009, Influence of plant communities on denitrification in a tidal freshwater marsh of the Potomac River, United States: Journal of Environmental Quality, v. 38, p. 618–626.

Johnson, T.C., 1980, Sediment redistribution by waves in lakes, reservoirs and embayments, *in* Stefan, H.G., ed., Proceedings of the Symposium on Surface Water Impoundments, American Society of Civil Engineers, vol. II: p. 1307–1317.

Johnston, D.W., 2000, The Dyke Marsh Preserve ecosystem: Virginia Journal of Science, v. 51, no. 4, p. 223–272.

Kjar, D.S., and Barrows, E.M., 2004, Arthropod community heterogeneity in a Mid-Atlantic forest highly invaded by alien organisms: Banisteria, v. 24, p. 26–37.

Kocin, P.J., Schumacher, P.N., Morales, R.F., Jr., and Uccellini, L.W., 1995, Overview of the 12–14 March 1993 superstorm: Bulletin of the American Meteorological Society, v. 76, no. 2, p. 165–182.

Komar, P.D., and Miller, M.C., 1973, The threshold of sediment movement under oscillatory waves: Journal of Sedimentary Petrology, v. 43, p. 1101–1110.

Komar, P.D., and Miller, M.C., 1975, On the comparison between the threshold of sediment motion under waves and unidirectional currents with a discussion on the practical evaluation of the threshold: Journal of Sedimentary Petrology, v. 45, p. 362–367.

Litwin, R.J., Smoot, J.P., Pavich, M.J., Markewich, H.W., Brook, G.A., and Verardo, S., 2010, Hybla cores 7 & 8—An 80,000-year Late Pleistocene climate record from the mid-Atlantic Coastal Plain of North America: Geological Society of America Abstracts with Programs, v. 42, no. 1, p. 151.

Madsen, J.D., Chambers, P.A., James, W.F., Koch, E.W., and Westlake, D.F., 2001, The interaction between water movement, sediment dynamics, and submersed macrophytes: Hydrobiologia, v. 444, no. 1–3, p. 71–84.

Markewich, H.W., Litwin, R.J., Pavich, M.J., and Brook, G.A., 2009, Late Pleistocene aeolian features in southeastern Maryland and the Chesapeake Bay region indicate strong WNW-NW winds accompanied growth of the Laurentide Ice Sheet: Quaternary Research, v. 71, no. 3, p. 409–425.

Myrick, R.M., and Leopold, L.B., 1963, Hydraulic geometry of a small tidal estuary: U.S. Geological Survey Professional Paper 422-B, 18 p.

National Oceanic and Atmospheric Administration, Coastal Services Center, 2010, Historical hurricane track graphics database. Maps and online database, accessed at http://csc-s-maps-q.csc noaa.gov/hurricanes/viewer html.

Normandeau Associates, Inc., 2009, Observations of erosion and deposition in Dyke Marsh Preserve (National Park Service), Alexandria, Virginia, 1992 to 2009, Final Report: Prepared for the National Park Service, George Washington Memorial Parkway, June 2009, Project No. 19190.016, 21 p.

Nyman, J.A., Walters, R.J., Delaune, R.D., and Patrick, W.H., Jr., 2006, Marsh vertical accretion via vegetative growth: Estuarine, Coastal and Shelf Science, v. 69, no. 3–4, p. 370–380.

Orth, R.J., Nowak, J.F., Wilcox, D.J., Whiting, J.R., and Nagey, L.S., 1998, Distribution of submerged aquatic vegetation in the Chesapeake Bay and tributaries and the Coastal Bays—1997: VIMS Special Scientific Report Number 138, Virginia Institute of Marine Science, Gloucester, VA, 144 p.

Palermo, M.R., and Ziegler, T.W., 1976, Feasibility study for Dyke Marsh demonstration area: Technical Report D-76-6, U.S. Army Corps of Engineers Dredged Material Research Program, Vicksburg, MS, 63 p.

Pasternak, G.B., and Brush, G.S., 2002, Biogeomorphic controls on sedimentation and substrate on a vegetated tidal freshwater delta in the upper Chesapeake Bay: Geomorphology, v. 43, no. 3–4, p. 293–311.

Pavich, M.J., Markewich, H.W., Litwin, R.J., Smoot, J.P., and Brook, G., 2010, Significance of marine oxygen isotope stage OIS5a and OIS3 OSL dates from estuarine sediments flanking Chesapeake Bay: Geological Society of America Abstracts with Programs, v. 42, no. 1, p. 101.

Reimer, P.J., Baillie, M.G.L., Bard, E., and others, 2004, IntCal04 terrestrial radiocarbon age calibration, 26-0 cal kyr BP: Radiocarbon, v. 46, no. 1029–1058.

Rowan, D.J., Kalff, J., and Rasmussen, J.B., 1992, Estimating the mud deposition boundary depth in lakes from wave theory: Canadian Journal of Fisheries and Aquatic Science, v. 49, p. 2490–2497.

Spencer, S.C., 2000, Population abundance and habitat requirements of the marsh wren (*Cistothorus palustris*) at Dyke Marsh National Wildlife Preserve—An urban conservation challenge: M.S. thesis, George Mason University, Fairfax,Virginia, 49 p.

Stevenson, J.C., Ward, L.G., and Kearney, M.S., 1988, Sediment transport and trapping in marsh systems—Implications of tidal flux studies: Marine Geology, v. 80, no. 1–2, p. 37–59.

Stuiver, M., and Reimer, P.J., 1993, Extended ^{14}C database and revised CALIB radiocarbon calibration program: Radiocarbon, v. 35, p. 215–230.

U.S. Army Coastal Engineering Research Center, 1972, Shore Protection Manual, v. 1, (3rd ed.): Washington, D.C., Government Printing Office, 714 p.

U.S. Army Coastal Engineering Research Center, 1984, Shore Protection Manual, v. 1, (4th ed.): Washington, D.C., Waterways Experiment Station, Corps of Engineers, Department of the Army, 598 p.

U.S. National Park Service, 2010, Dyke Marsh Wildlife Preserve: NPS map and pamphlet, accessed at http://www.nps.gov/gwmp/dyke-marsh htm.

Appendixes 1–5

Appendix 1.   Excerpts of Federal Legislation Ceding Dyke Marsh to the National Park Service, and Mandating Its Restoration

Appendix 1A.   Public Law 86-41 (1959, text)

Public Law 86-41
86th Congress, H.R. 2228
June 11, 1959

"To provide for the acquisition of additional land along the Mount Vernon Memorial Highway in exchange for certain dredging privileges, and for other purposes."

"Be it enacted by the Senate and House of Representatives of the United States of America in Congress assembled. That in order to protect more adequately the Mount Vernon Memorial Highway, to add further to its memorial character, and in order to acquire an area of irreplaceable wet lands near the Nation's Capitol which is valuable for the production and preservation of wildlife, the Secretary of the Interior is hereby authorized to carry out the following transactions with the Smoot Sand and Gravel Corporation:

(1) To accept on behalf of the United States of America... that piece of land lying on the east side of the Mount Vernon Memorial Highway and extending from approximately opposite station 459 to station 516+50, approximately five thousand seven hundred and fifty feet in length, and averaging approximately eight hundred feet in width, and containing one hundred and ten acres, more or less, and as further shown as area "A" on said plan.

(2) To accept on behalf of the United States of America...area "D" lying between area "A" and the Potomac River, and containing one hundred and fifty acres, more or less, the Smoot Sand and Gravel Corporation reserving unto itself, its successors and assigns, the right to remove sand and gravel there from for a period of thirty years, and for the same period reserving such riparian rights as may exist in area "D".

(3) To permit the Smoot Sand and Gravel Corporation, its successors and assigns, to remove sand and gravel from that part of United States property lying east of area "B" and opposite stations 426 to 459, to the extent of eighty-five acres, of the total one hundred and ten acres in area "C"...

(4) To require that the scope of dredging operations necessary to remove the sand and gravel in areas "C" and "D" be so limited and conducted as not to undermine the adjacent shores of areas "A" and "B";

(4)b ...so that these activities will be carried on in such a manner as to provide for the preservation of wildlife values in area "C" and "D"

(4)c ...The Secretary (of Interior) shall administer all of the lands described in this bill as "A", "B", "C" and "D" so that fish and wildlife development and their preservation as wetland wildlife habitat shall be paramount, except such portion thereof that the Secretary shall designate as part of the George Washington Memorial Parkway within one year from the effective date of this Act.

Approved June 11, 1959.

Appendix 1B. Public Law 86-41 (1959, accompanying map)

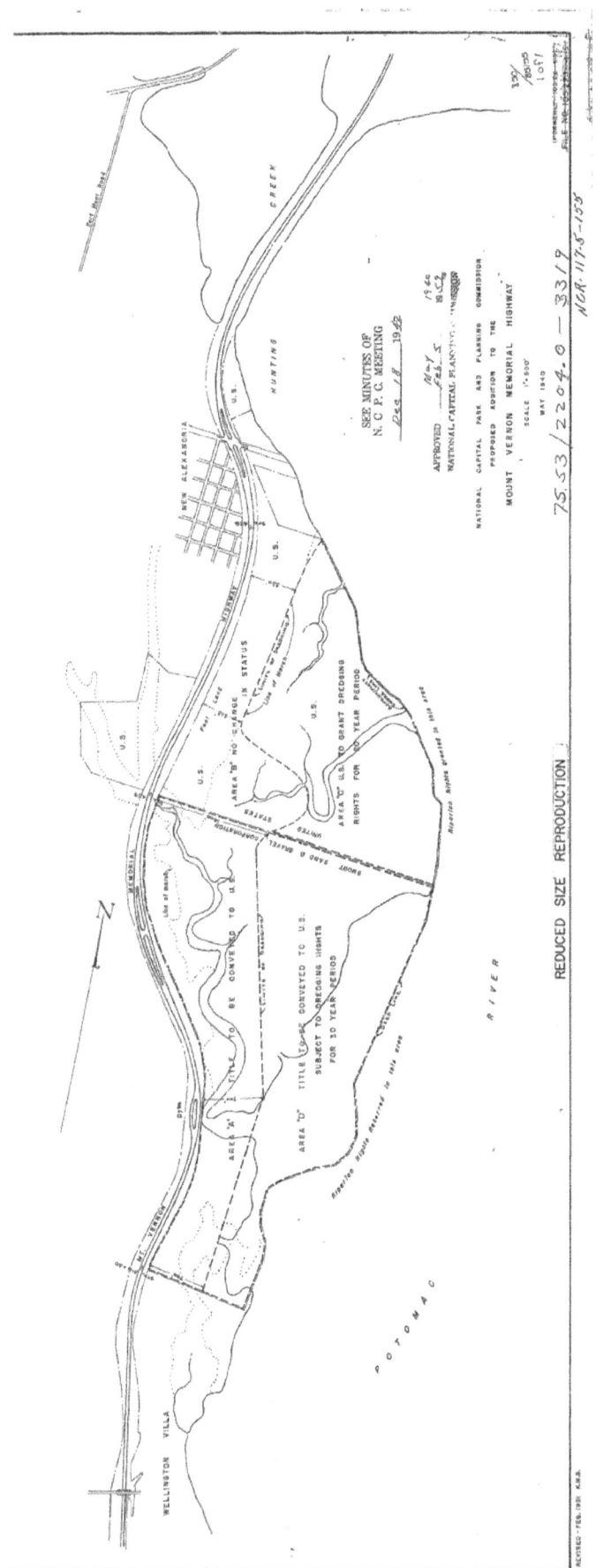

Appendix 1B.   Land acquisition map for Dyke Marsh (1959).

Appendix 1C.   Public Law 93-251 (excerpt)

Public Law 93-251
93rd Congress, H.R.10203
March 7, 1974
Title I - Water Resources Development
Section 86(a), page 26-27

"The Secretary of the Army, acting through the Chief of Engineers, is authorized to assist the National Park Service in the National Park Service's program to plan for, design, and implement restoration of the historical and ecological values of Dyke Marsh on the Potomac River."

Appendix 1D.   National Capital Region (NPS) archived image narrative 850-3014 (unpublished)

National Capital Region, National Park Service
Narrative—Dyke Marsh, GWMP, Section 5, part of the Master Plan
NCR scanned map collection, Map number 850-3014 (unpublished)
Date: unknown, (ca. 1964–1967).

Excerpt:

"The dredging for sand and gravel is being done by the Potomac Sand and Gravel Company* under terms of Public law 86-41 ... Through this dredging operation, sand and gravel is being removed from 235 acres of marsh and water, to a depth of approximately 30 feet below low water. "

*authors' note: The 1959 Public Law stipulates the mining agent as Smoot Sand and Gravel Company.

Appendix 2

Appendix 2A.   State rare plants and animals found at Dyke Marsh, with status codes

Ixobrychus exilis (least bittern), S3B/S3N, Dyke Marsh
Carex davisii (Davis' sedge), S1 G4
Schoenoplectus fluviatilis (river bullrush), S2 G5
Sparganium eurycarpum (Large Bur-reed), S3 G5
Epeolus howardi (bee), Dyke Marsh, new state record (2009)
Copestylum sexmaculata (flower fly), Dyke Marsh, new state record (2004)
Phrontosoma belfragei (sawfly), Dyke Marsh, new state record (2004)
Sialis iola (alderfly), Dyke Marsh, new state record (2004)
Sialis mohri (alderfly), Dyke Marsh, new state record (2004)

Appendix 2B.   Recent federally delisted birds found at Dyke Marsh, with status codes

Haliaeetus leucocephalus (American Bald Eagle) IUCN LC
Falco peregrinus (Peregrine Falcon) IUCN LC

Appendix 3.   Metadata for Imagery Used in This Report

Appendix 3A.   Metadata for photos used in figures (this report)

Item: Description:

1.   **Cover:** Hurricane Isabel.

Sensor: Aqua/MODIS

Start date: Sept. 17, 2003

Event Start date: Sept 8, 2003

NH Image ID: 11721

NH Event ID: 10151

NH Posting Date: Sept.17, 2003

Source: NASA GSFC, MODIS Rapid Response Team

Photo: Landsat 5 (visible)

Image source: Jacques Descloitres, Liam Gumley

UTC: 18:25

Link: http://vev2.gsfc nasa.gov/view_recphp?id=18886

Notes: 350 miles from mainland, NNW at 11 mph, sustained winds 105 mph

2.   **Figure 1B:** Dyke Marsh aerial imagery 2006 composite of USNG 18SUH210915 and USNG 18SUH210930.

Pub date: March 18, 2007

Title: High Resolution orthoimage USNG 18SUH210915 and USNG 18SUH210930, Prince George's Co., Maryland

Geoform: SDE raster digital data

Sername: USGS High Resolution State Orthoimagery

Issue: 1.0

Pubplace: SiouxFalls, SD

Publish: U.S. Geological Survey

Link: http://seamless.usgs.gov

Abstract: "Orthophotos combine the image characteristics of a photograph with the geometric qualities of a map. The primary digital orthophoto is a 30cm GSD resolution with tiles measuring 1500m x 1500m cast on the Universal Transverse Mercator projection (UTM) on the North American Datum of 1983 (NAD83/HARN). The aerial photography used to create the digital images was flown March 18th, 2006. The 2006 digital orthos were captured with an ADS40 sensor. The National Capital Planning Commission purchased RGB Natural Color orthophotography."

Note: The naming convention is based on the U.S. National Grid (USNG), taking the coordinates of the SW corner of the orthoimage.

Note: Visible low tide (~0 ft-1.5 ft above mean low water)

3.   **Figure 2A:** Dyke Marsh aerial photo 1937.

Photo date: April 30, 1937.

Image ID: FG 118 159

Other: #0848

Source: National Park Service.

Photo source: Air Survey Corporation

45180 Business Court

Loudon Gateway Center

Sterling VA 20166

(703) 471 4510

(reprinting)

Scale: approx 1 inch=1000 ft

Visible low tide (~0 ft-1.5 ft above mean low water)

Archive: George Washington Memorial Parkway Headquarters (GMWP), McLean, VA

4.   **Figure 2B:** Dyke Marsh aerial image 1938.

Photo date: May 1, 1938.

Image ID: AHV 3 117

Note: "Copy from the National Archives record group no. 145".

Visible low tide (~0 ft-1.5 ft above mean low water).

Source: U.S. National Archives

Image source: unattributed

Archive: George Washington Memorial Parkway Headquarters (GMWP), McLean, VA

5.   **Figure 2C:** 1864 bathymetry map of Potomac River.

Title: *Potomac River (in four sheets). Sheet No. 4. From Indian Head to Georgetown.*

Source: *Survey of the Coast of the United States.*

Pub. Date: 1864

Scale: 1/40,000.

Archive: Historical Map & Chart Collection, Office of Coast
        Survey, National Ocean Service, NOAA

Link: http://historicalcharts.noaa.gov

6.   **Figure 3:** Dyke Marsh aerial imagery 1959.

Photo date: Sept. 5, 1959.

Image ID: 1051 4 03

Source: National Park Service.

Photo source: Air Survey Corporation
        45180 Business Court
        Loudon Gateway Center
        Sterling, VA 20166
        (703) 471–4510

(reprinting)

Scale: approx 1 inch=1000 ft

Visible low tide (~0 ft-1.5 ft above mean low water)

Archive: George Washington Memorial Parkway Headquarters (GMWP), McLean, VA

7.   **Figure 5A:** 1883 bathymetry map of Potomac River.

Title: *Potomac River (in four sheets). Sheet No. 4. From Indian Head to Georgetown.*

Source: *Survey of the Coast of the United States. 4ᵗʰ Edition.*

Pub. Date: February 1883

Scale: 1:40,000.

Mapper: A.D. Bache

Archive: Historical Map & Chart Collection, Office of Coast Survey, National Ocean Service, NOAA

Link: http://historicalcharts.noaa.gov

8.   **Figure 5B:** 1906 bathymetry map of Potomac River.

Title: *Potomac River. Mattawoman Creek to Georgetown. Chart 560.*

Source: *Coast and Geodetic Survey of the United States.*

Pub. Date: February 1906

Projection: Polyconic

Scale: 1:40,000.

Mapper: unattributed

Archive: Historical Map & Chart Collection, Office of Coast Survey, National Ocean Service, NOAA

Link: http://historicalcharts.noaa.gov

9. **Figure 5C:** 1931 bathymetry map of Potomac River.

Title: Chart #560. The Potomac River from Mattawoman Creek to Georgetown.

Source: U.S. Coast and Geodetic Survey

Pub. date: July 13, 1931

Projection: unknown

Scale: 1:40,000

Mapper: U.S. Coast and Geodetic Survey

Archive: National Archives and Records Administration; partial copy in NPS

National Capital Region Map collection, #850-41029

10. **Figure 6A, B:** see item 3.

11. **Figure 6C, D:** see item 6.

12. **Figure 7A, B:** Dyke Marsh aerial imagery 1976.

Photo date: 1976.

Source: Palermo and Ziegler (1976, US Army Corps Engineers Technical Report D-76-6) Note: Visible low tide (~0'–1.5' above mean low water).

13. **Figure 7C, D:** Dyke Marsh aerial imagery 1987.

Photo date: Sept. 2, 1987.

Image ID: 003 008

UTC: 19:01

Scale: 1:12,000

Lat: none

Long: none

Film No.: 000000 004620 19 01 -- 60

Camera: WILD 15/ 4 UAGA-F, Nr.13108 153.23

Settings: 3D FS300, 1/450. f4.0

Other: 1294; 000084

Flight Line Protocol: per VIMS (Orth and others, 1998; see appendix 3B).

Source: U.S. Army Corps of Engineers, Baltimore District

Contact: Robert Blama

Note: Visible low tide (~0 ft-1.5 ft above mean low water)

Archive: George Washington Memorial Parkway Headquarters (GMWP), McLean, VA

14. **Figure 8A, B:** Dyke Marsh aerial imagery 2002 (composite of frames 8 and 10).

Photo date: November 14, 2002

Title: Potomac River DC-Bay

Scale: 1:12,000

UTC: 16:24:20

Image ID: 003 008

Lat: 38°45'24.2" N.

Long: 77°02'35.5" W.

Film number(s): 660370 AGFA 3614, 660370 AGFA 3615

Camera: WILD 15/ 4UAG-S, No.13258 152.99

Settings: 3D FS300, 1/450. f4.0

Other: FF--- EC---- dt012.0 CAM5242; 1269

Flight Line Protocol: Flight Line 3 per VIMS (See appendix 3B).

Source: U.S. Army Corps of Engineers, Baltimore District

Contact: Robert Blama

Note: Visible low tide (~0 ft-1.5 ft above mean low water)

Photo date: Nov. 14, 2002

Title: Potomac River DC-Bay

Scale: 1:12,000

UTC: 16:24:44

Image ID: 003 010

Lat: $38^0 46'35.1''$ N.

Long: $77^0 02'31.1''$ W.

Film number(s): 660370 AGFA 3610, 660370 AGFA 3611

Camera: WILD 15/ 4UAG-S, No.13258 152.99

Settings: 3D FS300, 1/450. f4.0

Other: FF--- EC---- dt012.0 CAM5242; 1271

Flight Line Protocol: Flight Line 3 per VIMS (See appendix 3B).

Source: U.S. Army Corps of Engineers, Baltimore District

Contact: Robert Blama

Note: Visible low tide (~0 ft-1.5 ft above mean low water)

15.   **Figure 8C, D:** See item #2

16.   **Figure 8E, F:** Overlay of items #3 and #5

17.   **Figure 9A:** see item #3

18.   **Figure 9B:** see item #6

19.   **Figure 9C:** see item #2

20.   **Figure 10A:** 1992 bathymetry inside Dyke Marsh boundary

Title: Hydrographic Chart, Dyke Marsh, Fairfax County

Author: Ocean Surveys, Inc.

91 Sheffield Street, Old Saybrook, CT 06475-2363

(860) 388-4631

Prepared for: George Washington Memorial Parkway, National Park Service

Publication Date: February 10, 1993

Project Manager: G.G. Reynolds

Drafted by: D.L. Bentley

Survey Date: December 16-19, 1992

Ocean Surveys Drawing Number: 92ES082

Scale: 1 inch = 200 inches

Contact for Copies: GWMP GIS, 703-289-2543

Link: http://www.oceansurveys.com

Archive: George Washington Memorial Parkway Headquarters (GMWP), McLean, VA

21.　　**Figure 10B:** 2009 bathymetry inside Dyke Marsh boundary

　　　　Title: DykeMarsh2009_PointData

　　　　Source: Normandeau Associates, Inc.

　　　　　　c/o William Ettinger

　　　　　　23723 Woods Drive

　　　　　　Lewes, DE 19958

　　　　　　302-945-3567

　　　　　　wettinger@normandeau.com

　　　　Prepared for: George Washington Memorial Parkway, National Park Service
Beginning date: Feb. 4, 2009.
Ending date: Feb. 10, 2009.
Currentness Reference: ground condition
Contact for Copies: GWMP GIS, 703-289-2543

　　　　Archive: George Washington Memorial Parkway Headquarters (GMWP), McLean, VA

　　　　Note: The conversion to MLW depths was based on use of Tidal Benchmark

　　　　　　Washington, D.C. (station 8594900), which has a MLW surface elevation value of 4.71 feet and an NAVD88 elevation value of 5.95 feet. To refer MLW to NAVD88, the following calculation was used. 4.71feet MLW –5.95 feet NAVD88 = –1.24 feet. The MLW_Depth field was calculated by subtracting the Elev_ft field from –1.24 feet.

22.　　**Figure 11A:** Bathymetry synthesis.

　　　　　　Source: see item #21 (Normandeau Associates, 2009)

23.　　**Figure 11B:** detail of breached peninsula at Hog Island Gut.

　　　　　　Photo date: Oct. 7, 1992.

　　　　　　Title: none

　　　　　　Scale: 1:12,000

　　　　　　UTC: 19:01

　　　　　　Image ID: 3- 7

　　　　　　Lat: none

　　　　　　Long: none

　　　　　　Frame number: 000070

　　　　　　Camera: unattributed

　　　　　　Other: -5132- 5 277 -66 125 ---- 0280 56-

　　　　　　　　------ 004285 1901—60 1351

　　　　　　Flight Line Protocol: Flight Line 3 per VIMS (Orth and others, 1998; See appendix 3B).

　　　　　　Source: U.S. Army Corps of Engineers, Baltimore District

　　　　　　Contact: Robert Blama

　　　　　　Note: Visible low tide (~0 ft-1.5 ft above mean low water)

24.　　**Figure 12A:** see item #13

25.　　**Figure 12B:** see item #14

26.　　**Figure 12C:** see item #2

27.　　**Figure 13:** see item #2

28.　　**Figure 14A:** see item #2

29.　　**Figure 14B:** see item #2

30.　　**Figure 18A:** see item #2

31.   **Figure 18B:** Enlargement of 2009 aerial photo of DMWP (south marsh).
Title: Aerial Imagery @2009 Commonwealth of Virginia
ID: DO_N16_8996_31
Latitude: 38⁰45'56.79"N.
Longitude: 77⁰02'51.06"W.
Source: Virginia Information Technologies Agency / Virginia Geographic Information Network
Scale: 1:12,000

32.   **Figure 18C:** Breach at south marsh
Source: this study
Latitude: 38⁰45'56.79"N.
Longitude: 77⁰02'51.06"W.
Photographer: Joseph P. Smoot (USGS)
Date: April 15, 2010.

33.   **Figure 18D:** see item #3
Latitude: 38⁰45'38.88"N.
Longitude: 77⁰02'49.13"W.

34.   **Figure 18E:** see item #6
Latitude: 38⁰45'38.88"N.
Longitude: 77⁰02'49.13"W.

35.   **Figure 18F:** see item #2
Latitude: 38⁰45'38.88"N.
Longitude: 77⁰02'49.13"W.

36.   **Figure19A:** see item #3

37.   **Figure 19B:** Oblique aerial photo of Dyke Marsh (facing westward)
ID: 070919JRP
Source: John Repetski (USGS)
Date: Sept. 19, 2007
UTC: 2230
Archive: George Washington Memorial Parkway Headquarters (GMWP), McLean, VA

38.   **Figure 20:** see item #2

39.   **Figure 22A:** see item #2

40.   **Figure 22B:** imbricated gravel on "Coconut Island"
Source: this study
Date: April 15, 2010
Image: Joseph P. Smoot (USGS)
Archive: George Washington Memorial Parkway Headquarters (GMWP), McLean, VA

41.   **Figure 22C:** exhumed tree roots
Source: this study
Date: April 15, 2010
Image: Joseph P. Smoot (USGS)
Archive: George Washington Memorial Parkway Headquarters (GMWP), McLean, VA

42.   **Figure 22D:** Debris throw on shoreline
Source: this study
Date: April 15, 2010
Image: Ron Litwin (USGS)
Archive: George Washington Memorial Parkway Headquarters (GMWP), McLean, VA

43.   **Figure 22E.** Denudation zone showed cannibalized marsh
                Source: this study
                Date: April 15, 2010
                Image: Joseph P. Smoot (USGS)
                Archive: George Washington Memorial Parkway Headquarters (GMWP), McLean, VA

44.   **Figure 23:** see item # 2, item #3, and item #14.

45.   **Figure 26A:** Eroding eastern shoreface of south marsh, facing south.
                Latitude: 38°45'53.04"N.
                Longitude: 77°02'51.82"W.
                Date: April 2010
                Source: this study
                Photo: Ron Litwin (USGS)

46.   **Figure 26 B:** see item #2

47.   **Figure 27 A:** see item #14

48.   **Figure 27 B:** see item #2

49.   **Appendix 5A:** Satellite view of winter storm (nor'easter).
        ID: 2016677
        Sensor: GOES-12 visible
        Date: Oct. 30, 1991.
        UTC: 12:26
        Dataset: NSS.HRPT.ND.D91303.S1226.E1238.B0239999.WI
        Source: NOAA-NASA GOES Project

50.   **Appendix 5B:** Satellite view of winter storm (nor'easter).
        Sensor: GOES-7 IR
        False color Infrared
        Date: Mar. 13, 1993.
        UTC: 10:01
        Source: NOAA-NASA GOES Project

51.   **Appendix 5C:** Satellite view of winter storm (nor'easter).
        Sensor: GOES visible satellite
        Date: Feb. 12, 2006.
        UTC: 12:45
        Source: NOAA-NASA GOES Project

52.   **Appendix 5D:** Satellite view of winter storm (nor'easter).
        Sensor: GOES visible satellite
        Date: April 16, 2007.
        UTC: 20:32
        Source: NOAA-NASA GOES Project

53.   **Appendix 5E:** Satellite view of winter storm (nor'easter).
        Sensor: GOES-12 visible
        Date: Nov. 12, 2009.
        UTC: 20:01
        Source: NOAA-NASA GOES Project

54.   **Appendix 5F:** Satellite view of winter storm (nor'easter).
        Sensor: GOES visible satellite

Date: Dec. 19, 2009.

UTC: 15:30

Source: NOAA-NASA GOES Project

55.   **Appendix 5G:** Satellite view of winter storm (nor'easter).

Sensor: GOES visible satellite

Date: Feb. 6, 2010.

UTC: 17:01

Source: NOAA-NASA GOES Project

Appendix 3B.   Specifications for acquiring aerial imagery (per VIMS protocol, Orth and others, 1998)

The protocol used by the U.S. Army Corps of Engineers (USACE) to acquire the imagery used in this report (photo years 1987 to 2002) followed the same guidelines in Orth and others (1998). The studies for which these USACE aerial photos originally were taken were focused on submersed aquatic vegetation (SAV). Although we have used this imagery for a derivative purpose (to quantify shoreline erosion), the imagery was applicable to both purposes because of its high resolution and clarity.

Guidelines for aerial photographs:

1. Scale: 1/12,000 (VIMS scale is 1/24,000).

2. Tidal Stage: Photography was acquired at low tide, ~0 ft-1.5 ft above mean low water, as predicted by National Ocean Survey tables.

3. Plant growth: Imagery was acquired when growth stages ensured maximum delineation of SAV, aand when phonologic stage overlap was greatest.

4. Sun angle: Photography was acquired when surface reflection from sun glint did not cover more than 30 percent of frame. Sun angle generally was between 20^0 and 40^0 to minimize water surface glitter. At least 60 percent line overlap and 20 percent side lap were used to minimize image degradation due to sun glint.

5. Turbidity: Photography was acquired when clarity of water ensured complete delineation of grass beds. This was determined visually from the airplane to insure that SAV could be seen by the observer.

6. Wind: Photography was acquired during periods of no or low wind. Offshore winds were preferred to onshore winds when wind conditions could not be avoided.

7. Atmospherics: Photography was acquired during periods of no or low haze and (or) clouds below aircraft. There could be no more than scattered or thin broken clouds, or thin overcast above aircraft, to ensure maximum SAV contrast to bottom.

8. Sensor operation: Photography was acquired in the vertical mode with less than 5 degrees tilt. Scale/altitude/film/focal length combination permitted resolution of [a minimum of] 1 square meter of SAV (at the surface).

9. Plotting: Each flight line included sufficient identifiable land area to assure accurate plotting of grass beds.

Note: We confirmed the tidal stage of older existing aerial photography used in this study by several other criteria. A persistent landform within the Hog Island Gut (fig.1, 'LTI') served as a functional indicator of tidal stage. Field experience determined that it was emergent during low tide and fully inundated during high tide. Flooding, or the lack of it, within the distal tributaries of the marsh (second- and third-order distal tributaries) also served as a visual indicator of tidal stage. Lastly, more recent photos of the marsh (2002, 2006, and 2009) clearly show the shoreward 'rip-up' zone (vertical scour zone) to be fully exposed eastward of the marsh edge at low water conditions.

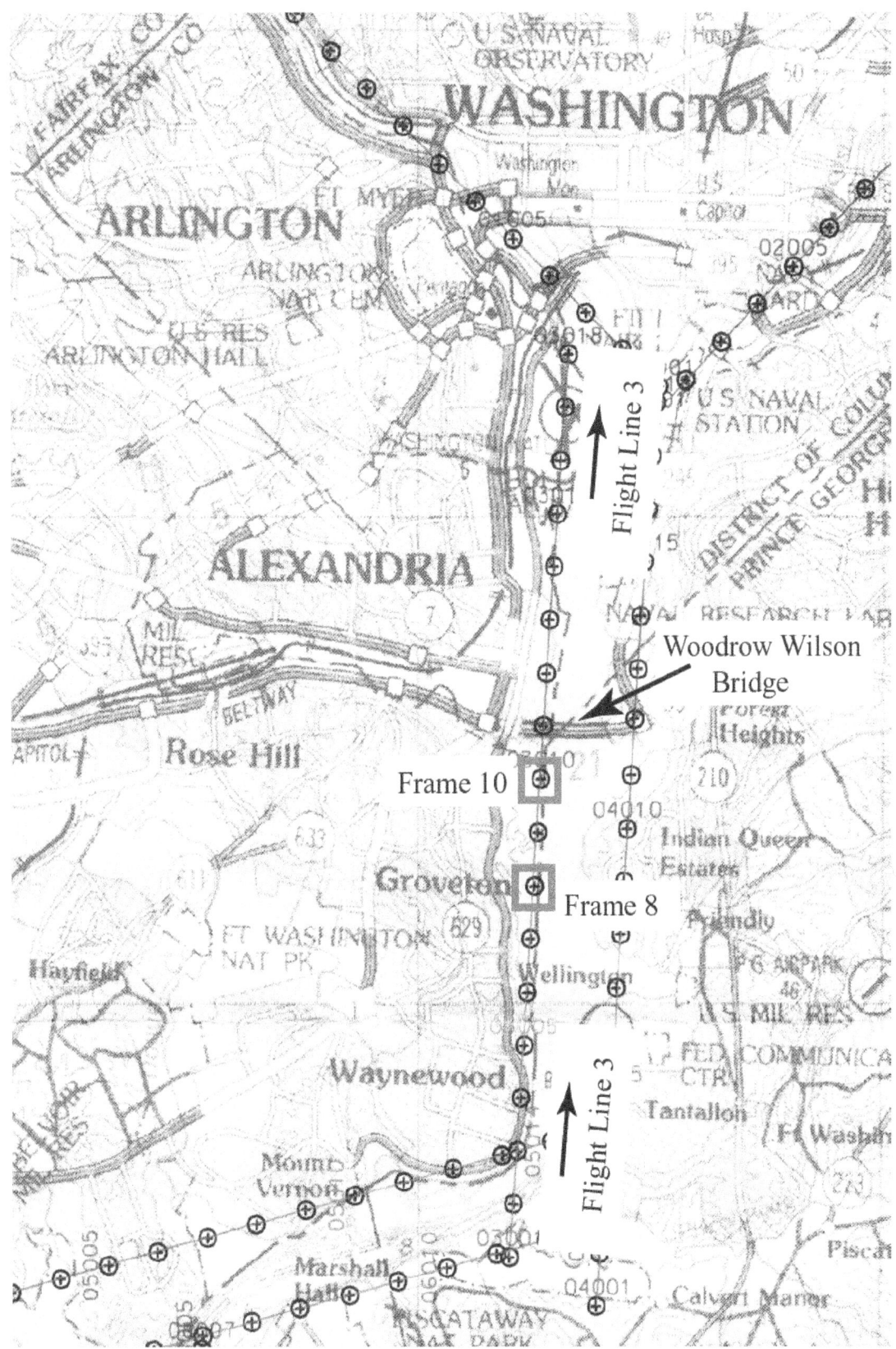

Appendix 3C. Map of aerial photography flight line (and frames used) to acquire imagery (Flight Line 3).

Appendix 4. Tracks of tropical depressions, tropical storms, and hurricanes (warm-cored storms) that likely induced erosion at Dyke Marsh (1939–2009).

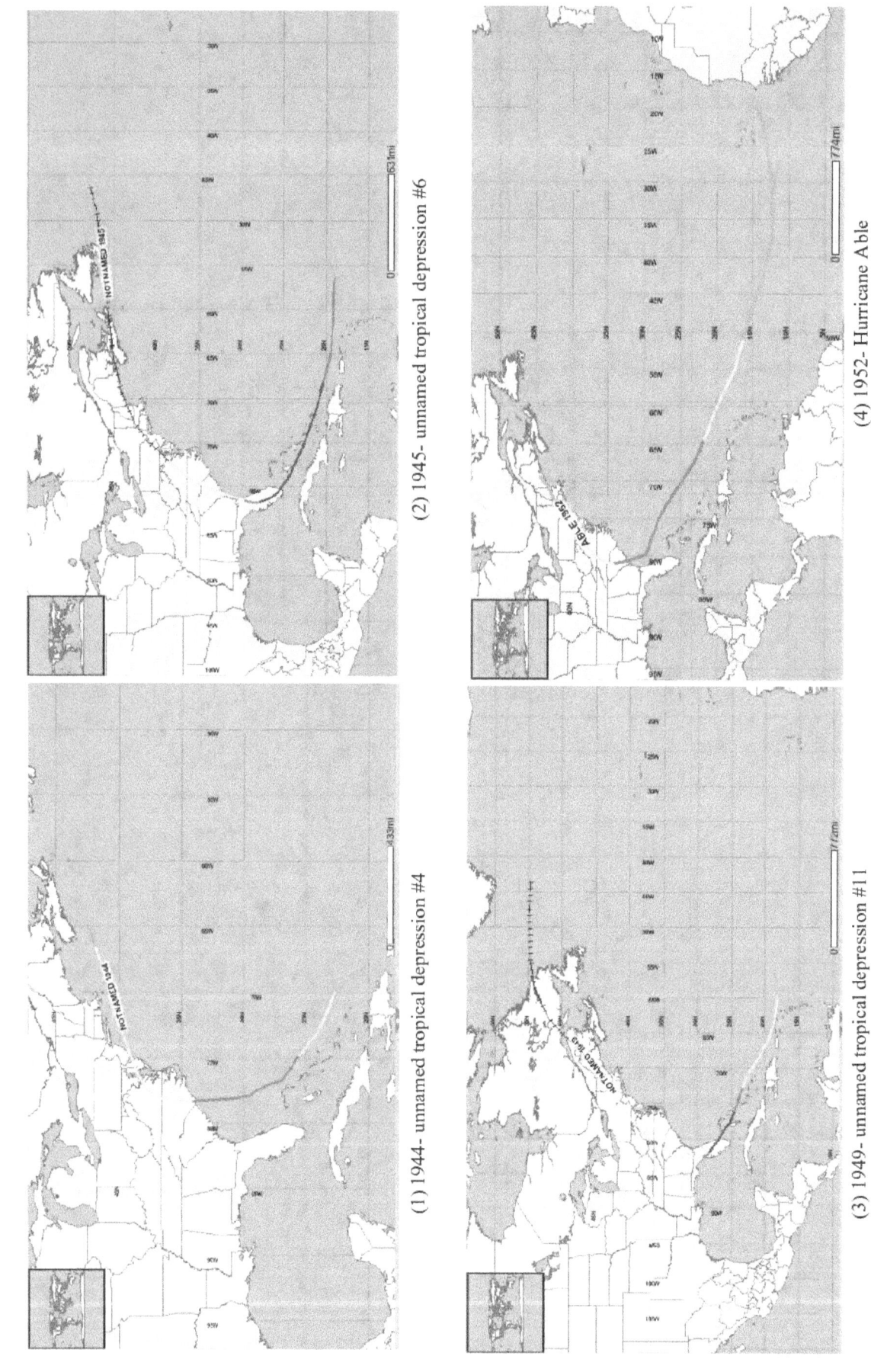

(1) 1944- unnamed tropical depression #4

(2) 1945- unnamed tropical depression #6

(3) 1949- unnamed tropical depression #11

(4) 1952- Hurricane Able

Appendix 4A.   Tropical depressions (summer storms) with high probability of causing shoreline erosion at Dyke Marsh. [Graphics courtesy of NOAA (2010) (NOAA hurricane viewer). Tracks are color coded to reflect wind-based storm strength. Green= tropical depression, Yellow= tropical storm, Orange = Category 1–2 hurricane, Red = category 3–5 hurricane, and +++ = extratropical storm.]

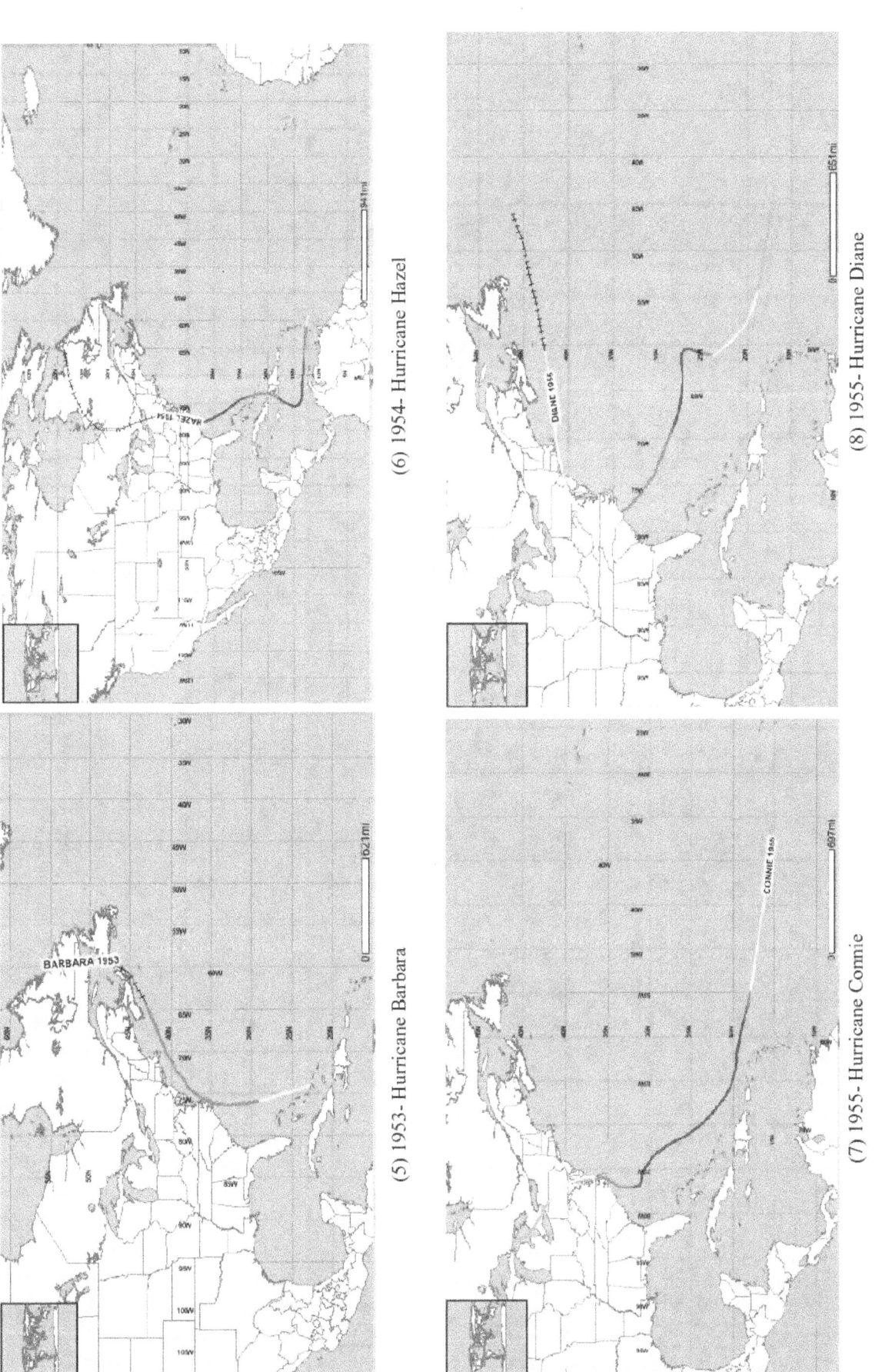

(6) 1954- Hurricane Hazel

(8) 1955- Hurricane Diane

(5) 1953- Hurricane Barbara

(7) 1955- Hurricane Connie

(data source: NOAA Coastal Services Center, http://csc-s-maps-q.csc noaa.gov/hurricanes/viewer html)

Appendix 4A.   Tropical depressions (summer storms) with high probability of causing shoreline erosion at Dyke Marsh.—Continued
[Graphics courtesy of NOAA (2010) (NOAA hurricane viewer). Tracks are color coded to reflect wind-based storm strength. Green= tropical depression, Yellow= tropical storm, Orange = Category 1–2 hurricane, Red = category 3–5 hurricane, and +++ = extratropical storm.]

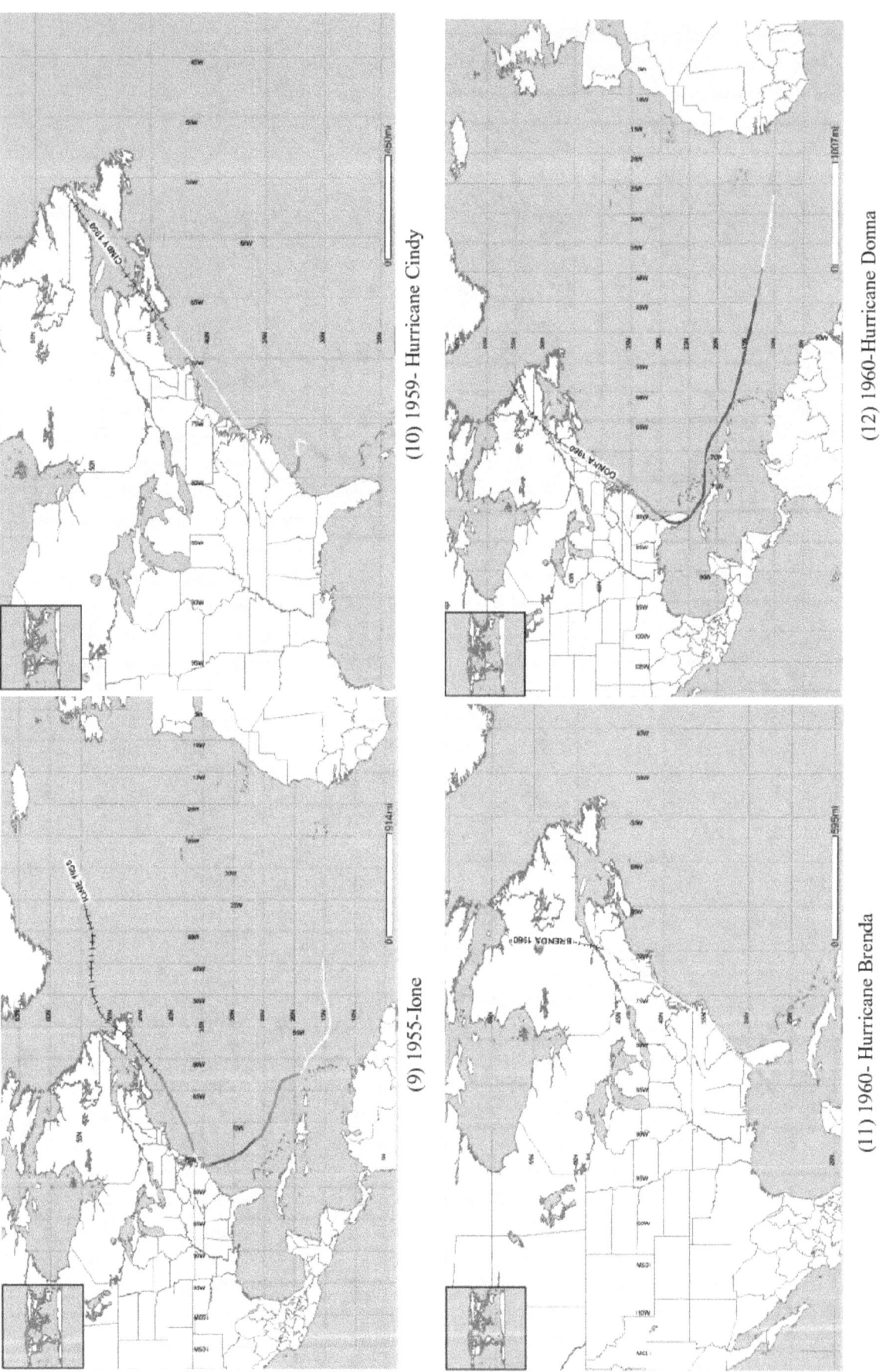

(10) 1959- Hurricane Cindy

(9) 1955-Ione

(12) 1960-Hurricane Donna

(11) 1960 - Hurricane Brenda

(data source: NOAA Coastal Services Center, http://csc-s-maps-q.csc noaa.gov/hurricanes/viewer.html)

Appendix 4A. Tropical depressions (summer storms) with high probability of causing shoreline erosion at Dyke Marsh.—Continued

[Graphics courtesy of NOAA (2010) (NOAA hurricane viewer). Tracks are color coded to reflect wind-based storm strength. Green= tropical depression, Yellow= tropical storm, Orange = Category 1–2 hurricane, Red = category 3–5 hurricane, and +++ = extratropical storm.]

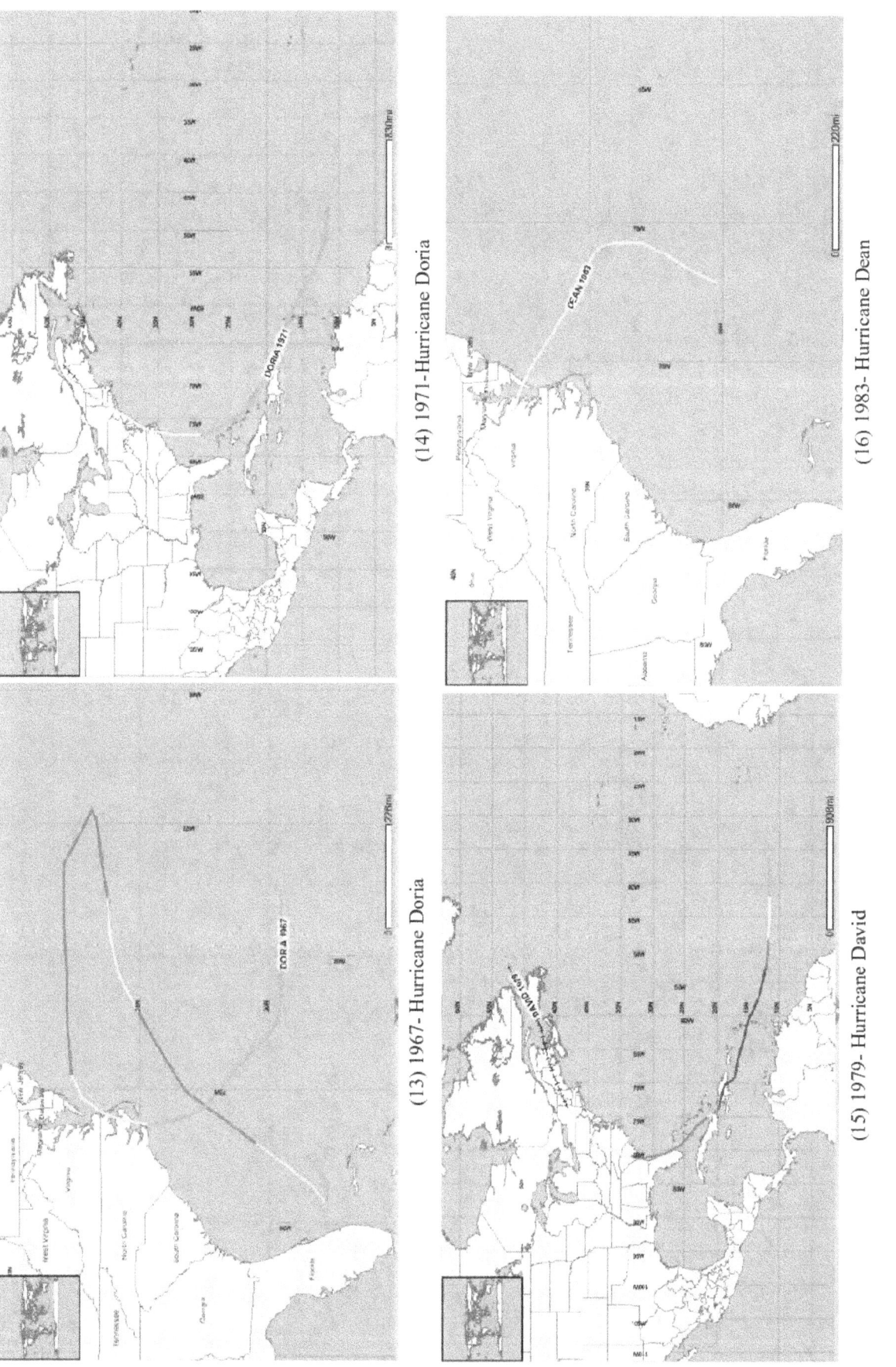

(13) 1967- Hurricane Doria

(14) 1971-Hurricane Doria

(15) 1979- Hurricane David

(16) 1983- Hurricane Dean

(data source: NOAA Coastal Services Center, http://csc-s-maps-q.csc.noaa.gov/hurricanes/viewer.html)

Appendix 4A.   Tropical depressions (summer storms) with high probability of causing shoreline erosion at Dyke Marsh.—Continued

[Graphics courtesy of NOAA (2010) (NOAA hurricane viewer). Tracks are color coded to reflect wind-based storm strength. Green=tropical depression, Yellow= tropical storm, Orange = Category 1–2 hurricane, Red = category 3–5 hurricane, and +++ = extratropical storm.]

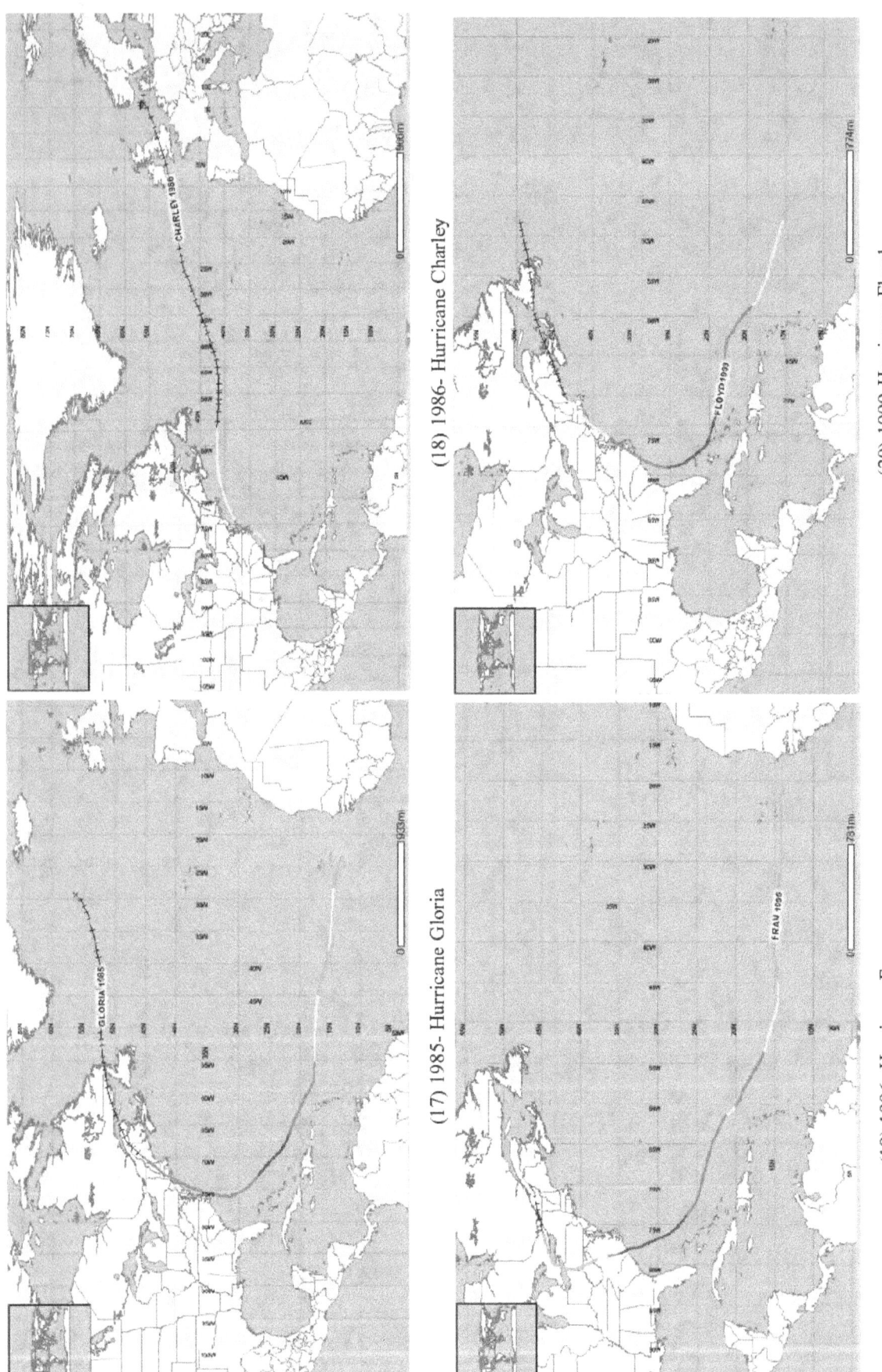

(17) 1985- Hurricane Gloria

(18) 1986- Hurricane Charley

(19) 1996- Hurricane Fran

(20) 1999- Hurricane Floyd

Appendix 4A.   Tropical depressions (summer storms) with high probability of causing shoreline erosion at Dyke Marsh.—Continued

[Graphics courtesy of NOAA (2010) (NOAA hurricane viewer). Tracks are color coded to reflect wind-based storm strength. Green= tropical depression, Yellow= tropical storm, Orange = Category 1–2 hurricane, Red = category 3–5 hurricane, and +++ = extratropical storm.]

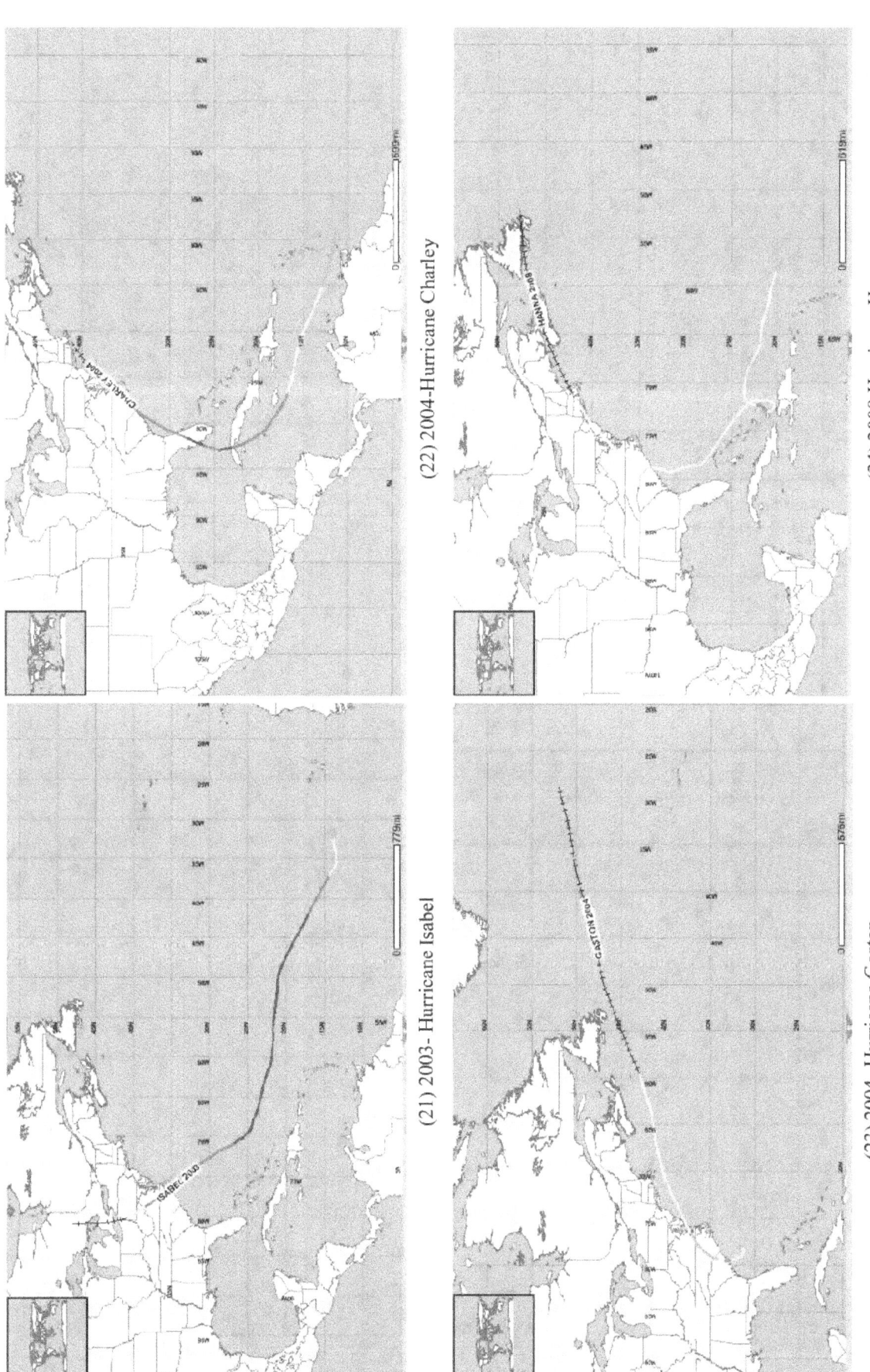

(21) 2003- Hurricane Isabel

(22) 2004-Hurricane Charley

(23) 2004- Hurricane Gaston

(24) 2008-Hurricane Hanna

(data source: NOAA Coastal Services Center, http://csc-s-maps-q.csc.noaa.gov/hurricanes/viewer.html)

Appendix 4A.   Tropical depressions (summer storms) with high probability of causing shoreline erosion at Dyke Marsh.—Continued
[Graphics courtesy of NOAA (2010) (NOAA hurricane viewer). Tracks are color coded to reflect wind-based storm strength. Green= tropical depression, Yellow= tropical storm, Orange = Category 1–2 hurricane, Red = category 3–5 hurricane, and +++ = extratropical storm.]

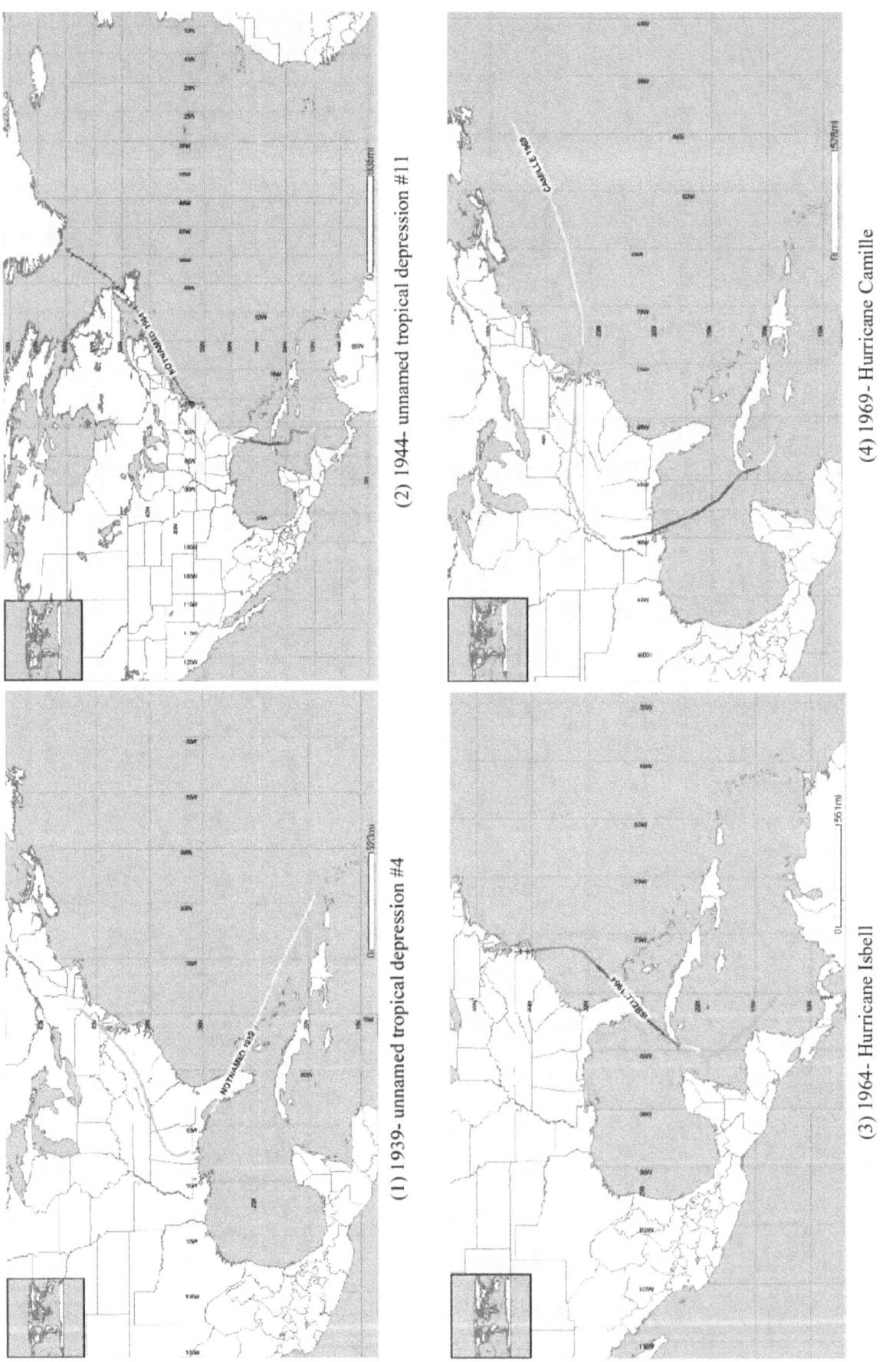

(1) 1939- unnamed tropical depression #4

(2) 1944- unnamed tropical depression #11

(3) 1964- Hurricane Isbell

(4) 1969- Hurricane Camille

(data source: NOAA Coastal Services Center, http://csc-s-maps-q.csc noaa.gov/hurricanes/viewer html)

Appendix 4B.   Tropical depressions (summer storms) with medium probability of causing shoreline erosion at Dyke Marsh.
[Graphics courtesy of NOAA (2010) (NOAA hurricane viewer). Tracks are color coded to reflect wind-based storm strength. Green= tropical depression, Yellow= tropical storm, Orange = Category 1–2 hurricane, Red = category 3–5 hurricane, and +++ = extratropical storm.]

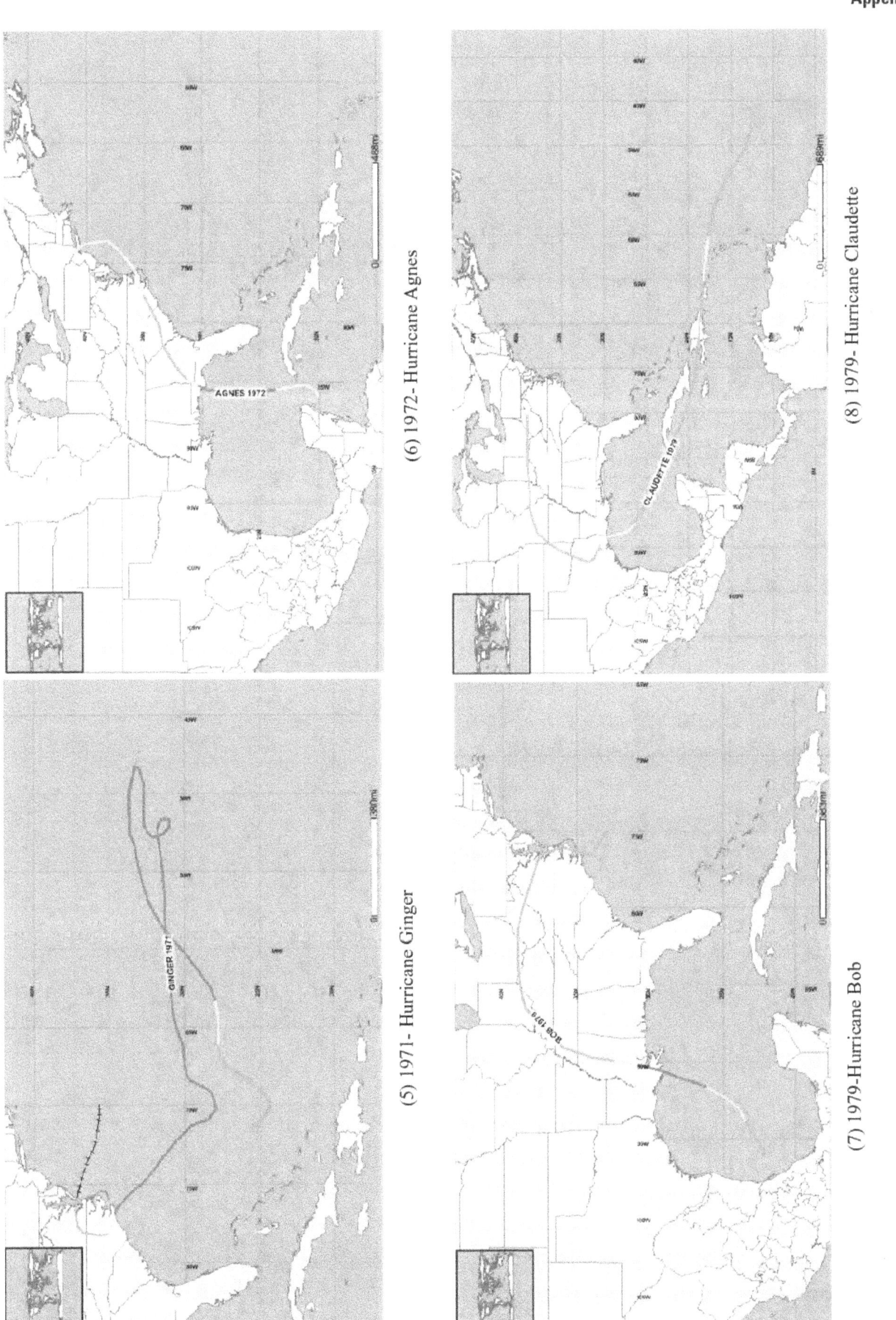

(5) 1971- Hurricane Ginger

(6) 1972- Hurricane Agnes

(7) 1979-Hurricane Bob

(8) 1979- Hurricane Claudette

(data source: NOAA Coastal Services Center, http://csc-s-maps-q.csc.noaa.gov/hurricanes/viewer.html)

Appendix 4B.   Tropical depressions (summer storms) with medium probability of causing shoreline erosion at Dyke Marsh.—Continued

[Graphics courtesy of NOAA (2010) (NOAA hurricane viewer). Tracks are color coded to reflect wind-based storm strength. Green= tropical storm. Green= tropical depression, Yellow= tropical storm, Orange = Category 1–2 hurricane, Red = category 3–5 hurricane, and +++ = extratropical storm.]

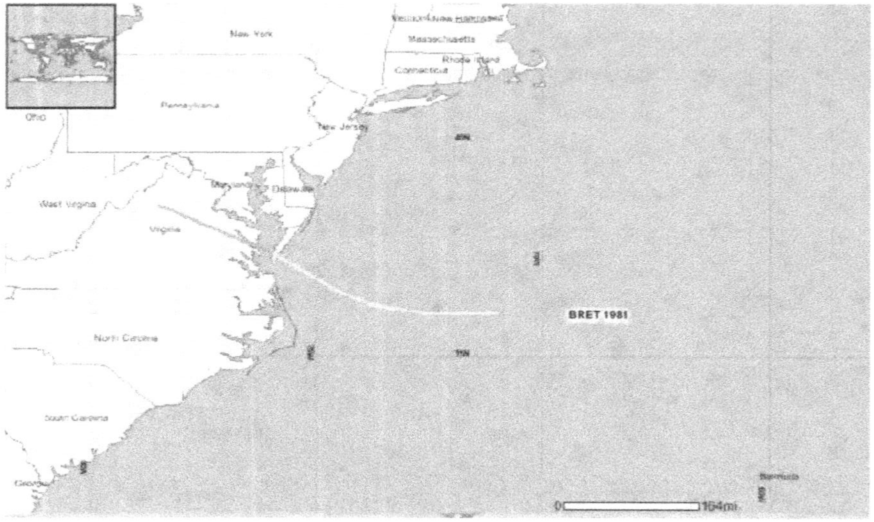

(10) 1985- Hurricane Bob

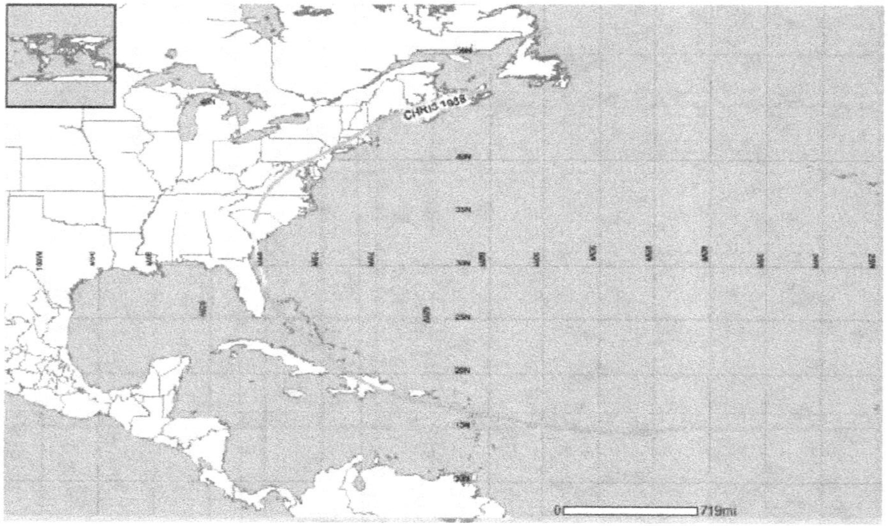

(12) 1988- Tropical Storm Chris

(9) 1981- Hurricane Bret

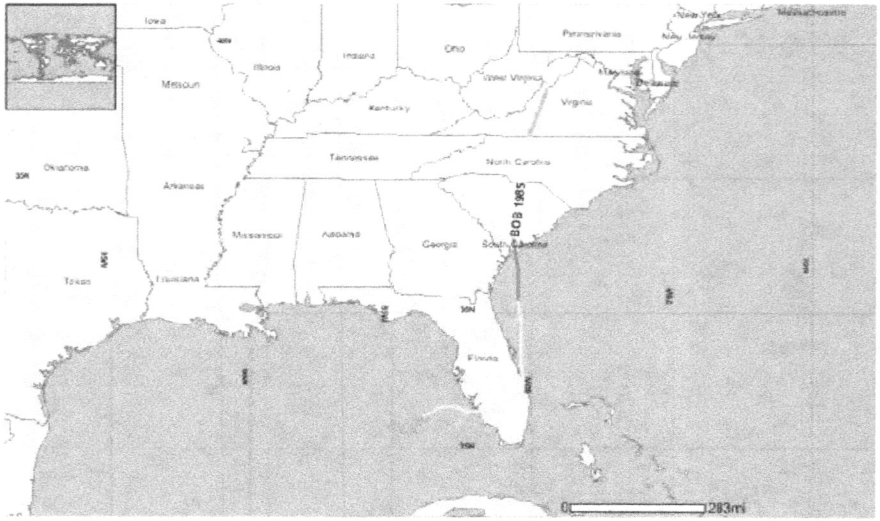

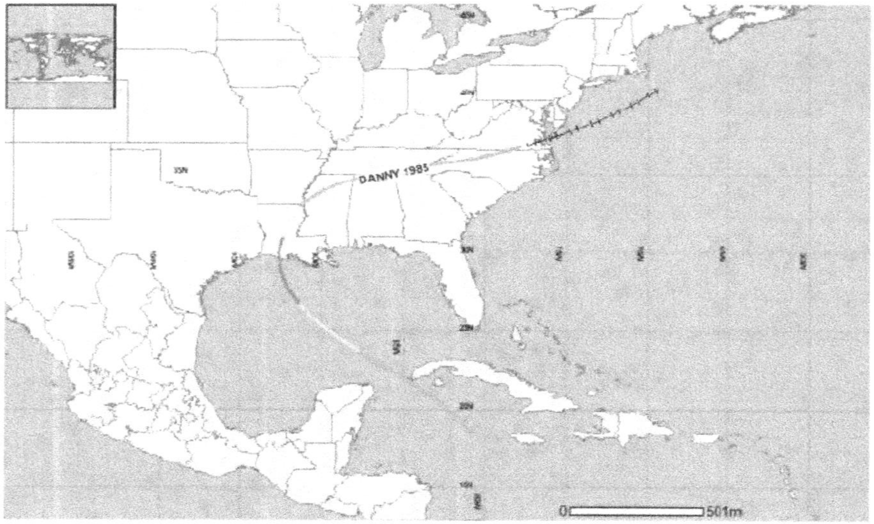

(11) 1985-Hurricane Danny

(data source: NOAA Coastal Services Center, http://csc-s-maps-q.csc noaa.gov/hurricanes/viewer html)

Appendix 4B.   Tropical depressions (summer storms) with medium probability of causing shoreline erosion at Dyke Marsh.—Continued
[Graphics courtesy of NOAA (2010) (NOAA hurricane viewer). Tracks are color coded to reflect wind-based storm strength. Green= tropical depression, Yellow= tropical storm, Orange = Category 1–2 hurricane, Red = category 3–5 hurricane, and +++ = extratropical storm.]

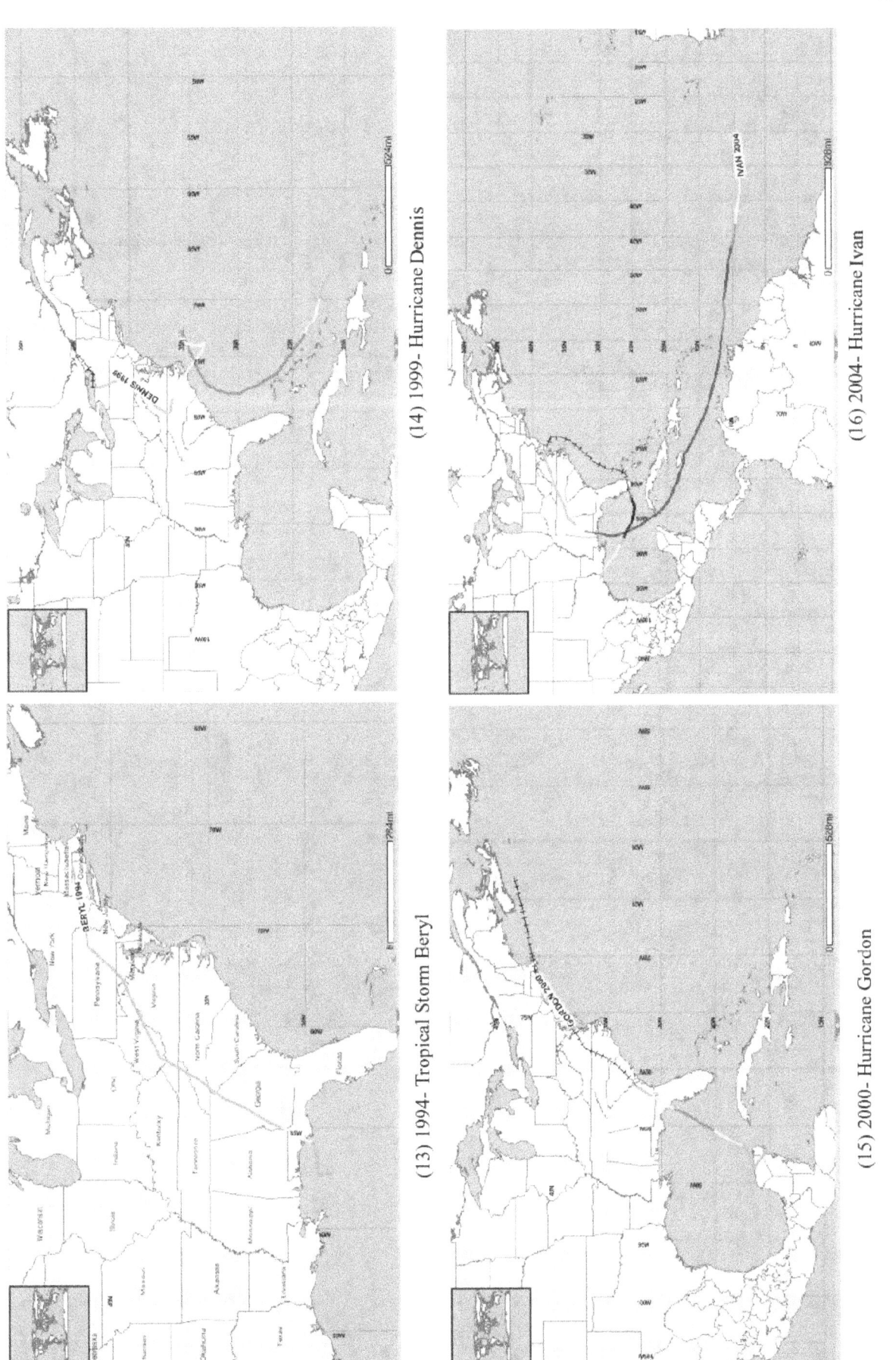

(14) 1999- Hurricane Dennis

(16) 2004- Hurricane Ivan

(13) 1994- Tropical Storm Beryl

(15) 2000- Hurricane Gordon

(data source: NOAA Coastal Services Center, http://csc-s-maps-q.csc noaa.gov/hurricanes/viewer.html)

Appendix 4B. Tropical depressions (summer storms) with medium probability of causing shoreline erosion at Dyke Marsh.—Continued

[Graphics courtesy of NOAA (2010) (NOAA hurricane viewer). Tracks are color coded to reflect wind-based storm strength. Green=tropical depression, Yellow= tropical storm, Orange = Category 1–2 hurricane, Red = category 3–5 hurricane, and +++ = extratropical storm.]

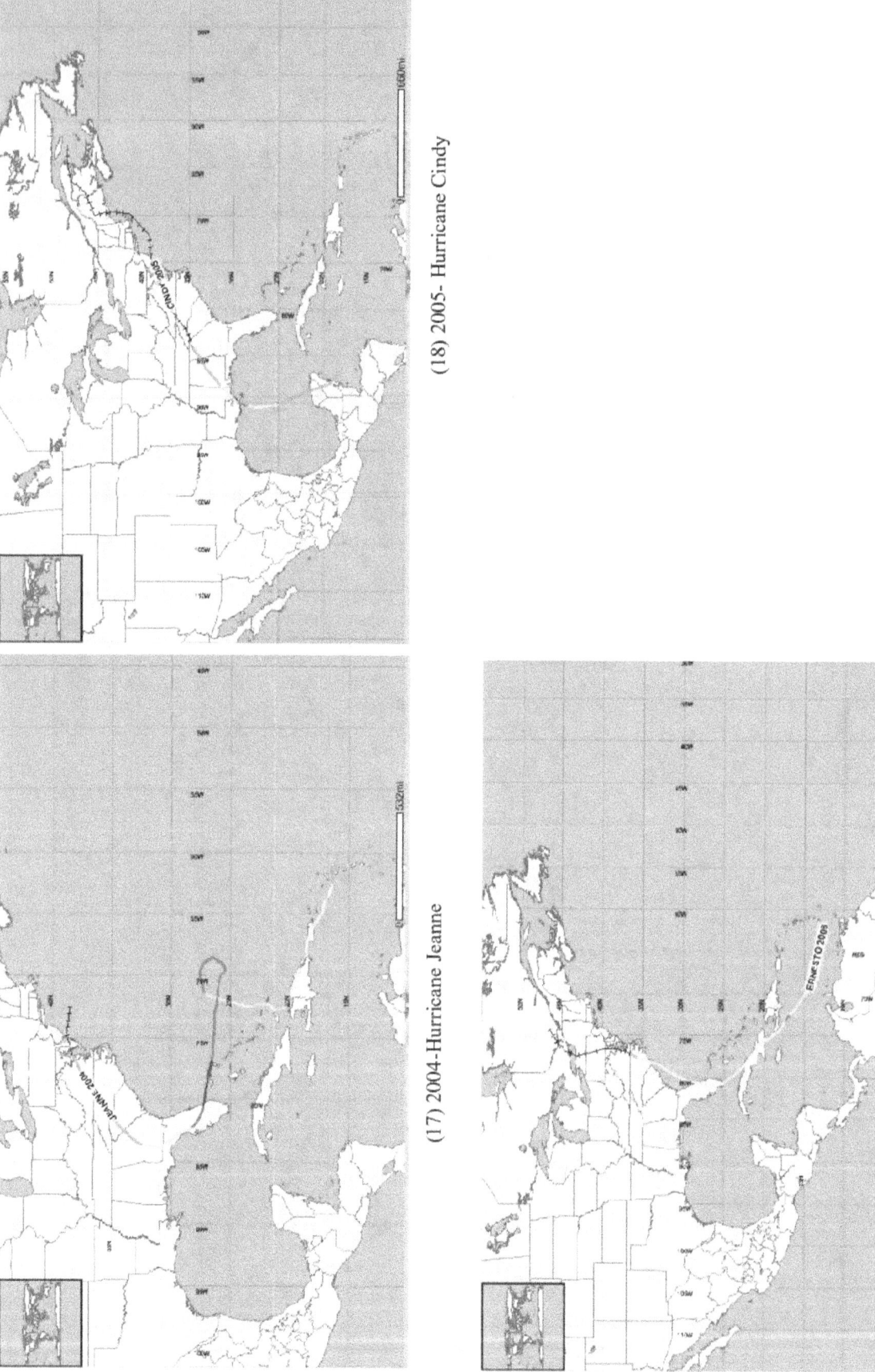

(17) 2004-Hurricane Jeanne

(18) 2005- Hurricane Cindy

(19) 2006- Hurricane Ernesto

(data source: NOAA Coastal Services Center, http://csc-s-maps-q.csc noaa.gov/hurricanes/viewer html)

Appendix 4B.   Tropical depressions (summer storms) with medium probability of causing shoreline erosion at Dyke Marsh.—Continued

[Graphics courtesy of NOAA (2010) (NOAA hurricane viewer). Tracks are color coded to reflect wind-based storm strength. Green= tropical depression, Yellow= tropical storm, Orange = Category 1–2 hurricane, Red = category 3–5 hurricane, and +++ = extratropical storm.]

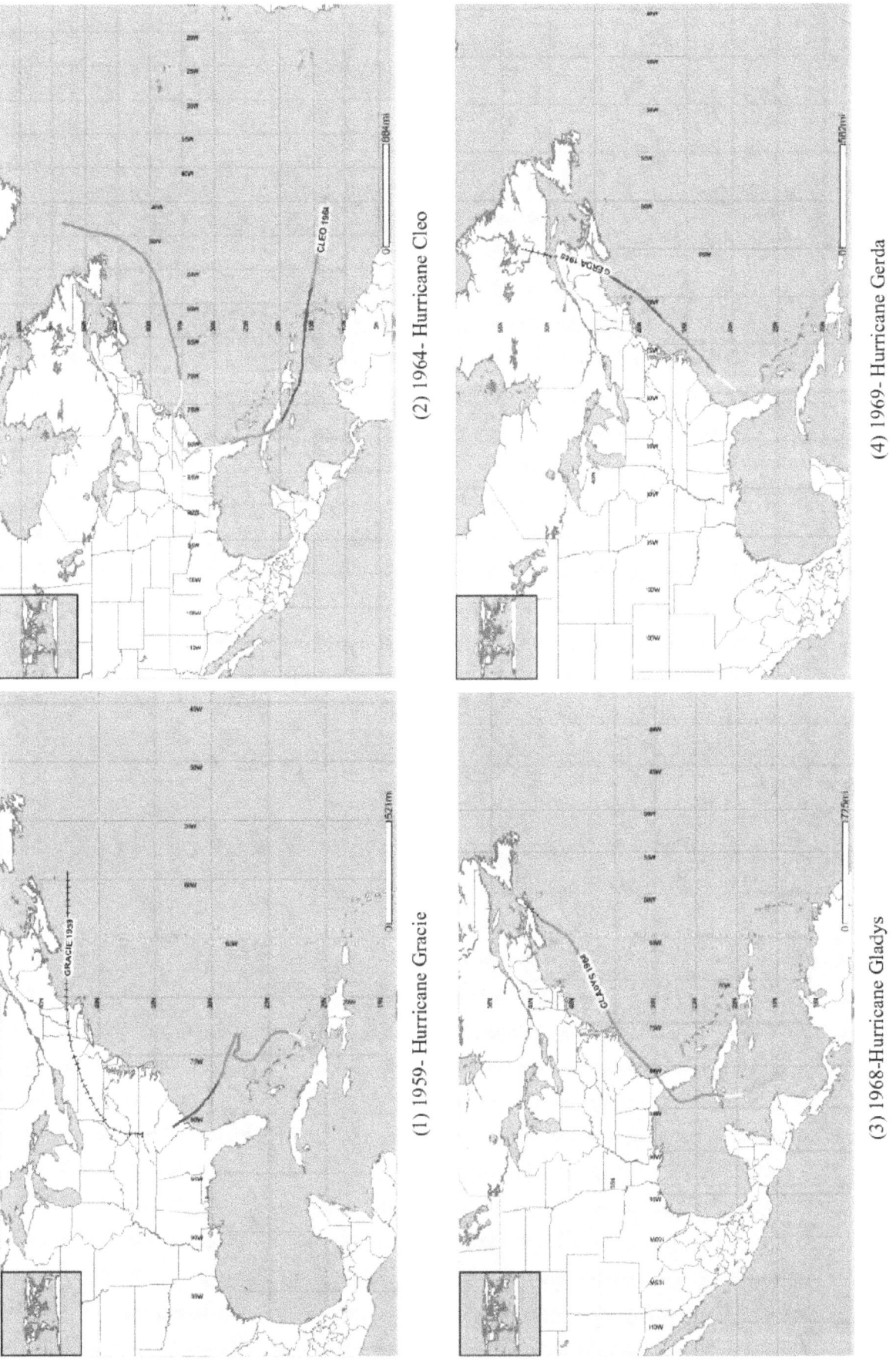

(2) 1964- Hurricane Cleo

(4) 1969- Hurricane Gerda

(1) 1959- Hurricane Gracie

(3) 1968-Hurricane Gladys

Appendix 4C.   Tropical depressions (summer storms) that possibly caused shoreline erosion at Dyke Marsh.

[Graphics courtesy of NOAA (2010) (NOAA hurricane viewer). Tracks are color coded to reflect wind-based storm strength. Green= tropical depression, Yellow= tropical storm, Orange = Category 1–2 hurricane, Red = category 3–5 hurricane, and +++ = extratropical storm.]

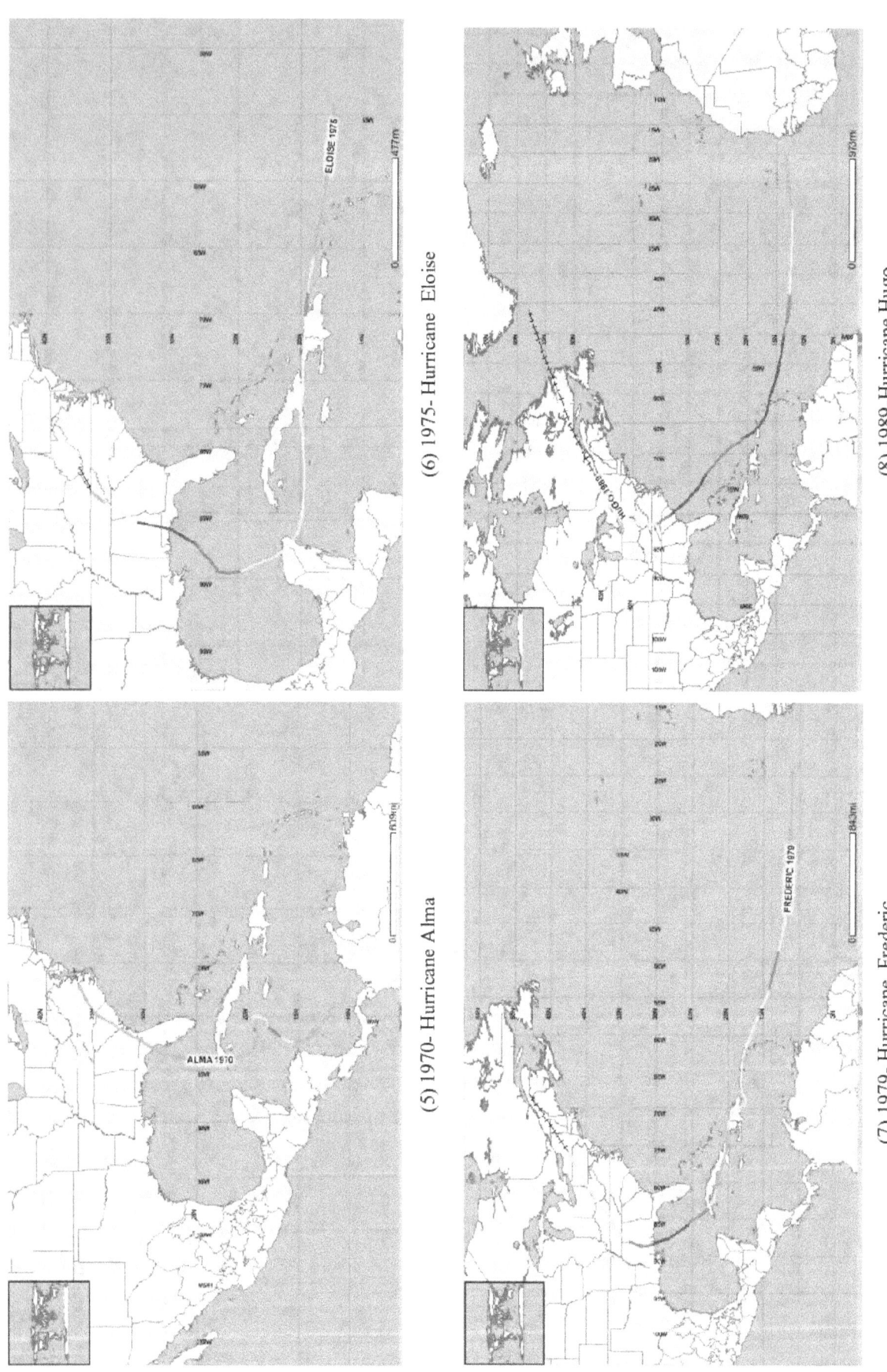

(6) 1975- Hurricane Eloise

(8) 1989-Hurricane Hugo

(5) 1970- Hurricane Alma

(7) 1979- Hurricane Frederic

Appendix 4C.   Tropical depressions (summer storms) that possibly caused shoreline erosion at Dyke Marsh.—Continued

(data source: NOAA Coastal Services Center, http://csc-s-maps-q.csc.noaa.gov/hurricanes/viewer.html)

[Graphics courtesy of NOAA (2010) (NOAA hurricane viewer). Tracks are color coded to reflect wind-based storm strength. Green= tropical depression, Yellow= tropical storm, Orange = Category 1–2 hurricane, Red = category 3–5 hurricane, and ++ = extratropical storm.]

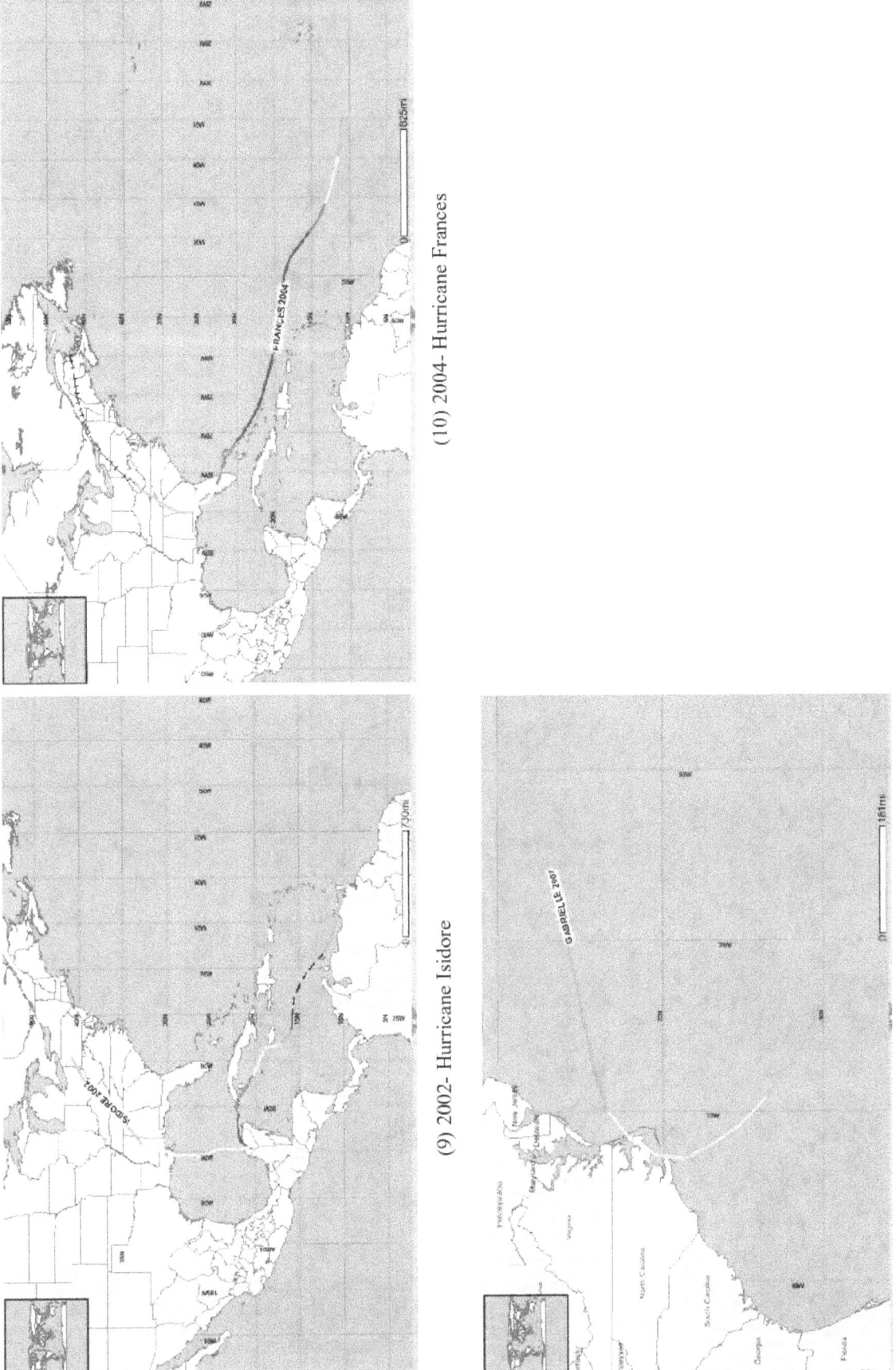

(10) 2004- Hurricane Frances

(9) 2002- Hurricane Isidore

(11) 2007- Hurricane Gabrielle

Appendix 4C.   Tropical depressions (summer storms) that possibly caused shoreline erosion at Dyke Marsh.—Continued

[Graphics courtesy of NOAA (2010) (NOAA hurricane viewer). Tracks are color coded to reflect wind-based storm strength. Green= tropical depression, Yellow= tropical storm, Orange = Category 1–2 hurricane, Red = category 3–5 hurricane, and +++ = extratropical storm.]

(data source: NOAA Coastal Services Center, http://csc-s-maps-q.csc noaa.gov/hurricanes/viewer html)

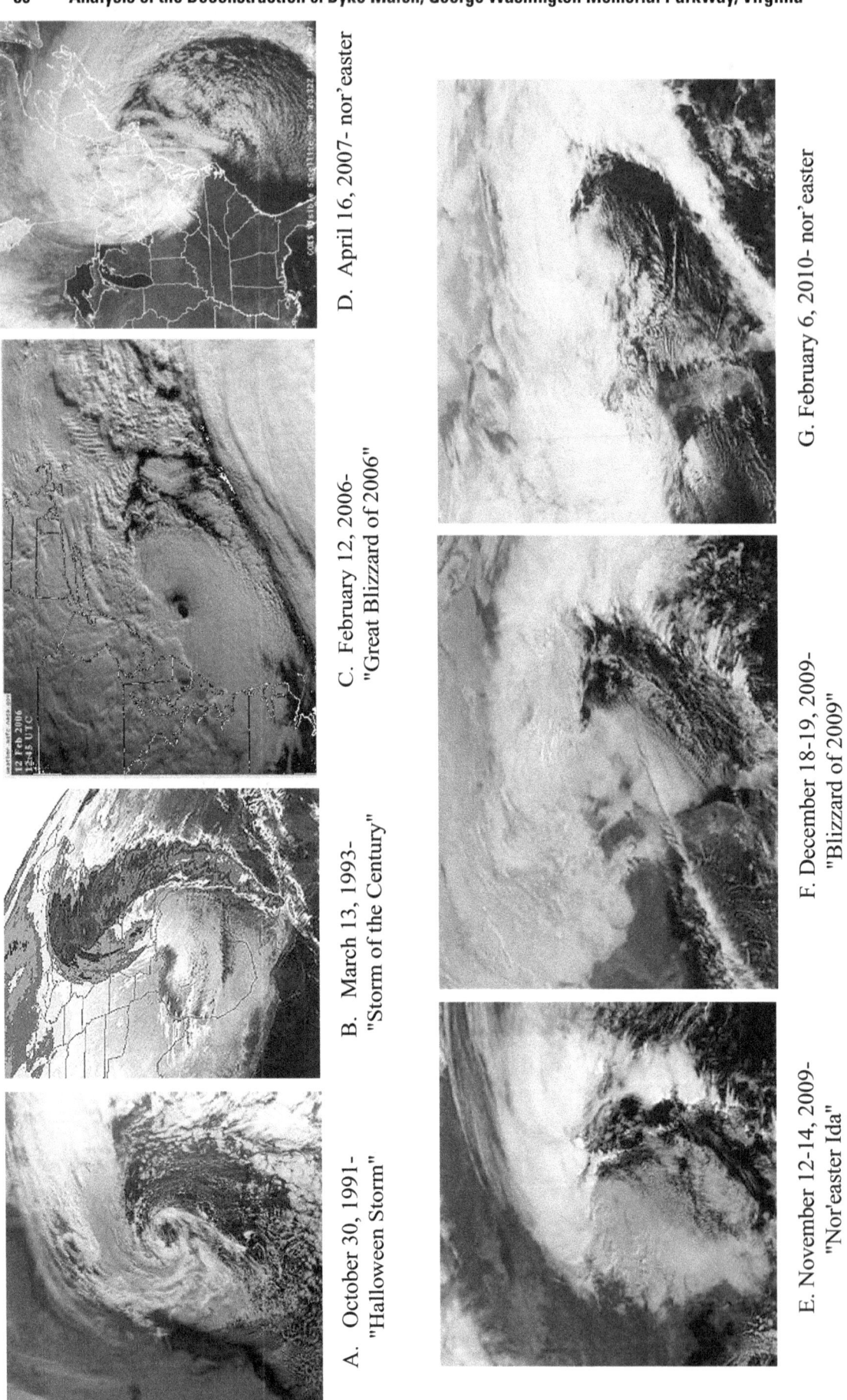

A. October 30, 1991- "Halloween Storm"

B. March 13, 1993- "Storm of the Century"

C. February 12, 2006- "Great Blizzard of 2006"

D. April 16, 2007- nor'easter

E. November 12-14, 2009- "Nor'easter Ida"

F. December 18-19, 2009- "Blizzard of 2009"

G. February 6, 2010- nor'easter

Appendix 5. Winter (cold-cored) storms that likely induced shoreline erosion at Dyke Marsh. [Note that nor'easters appear to be both frequent and damaging storm events at Dyke Marsh.] A, Satellite imagery- nor'easter of October 30, 1991; "Halloween Storm" (photo: NOAA-NASA GOES Project). B, Colorized infra-red satellite imagery- nor'easter of March 13, 1993; "Storm of the Century" (photo: NOAA-NASA GOES Project). C, Visible satellite imagery- nor'easter of February 12, 2006; "Great Blizzard of 2006" (photo: NOAA-NASA GOES Project). D, Visible satellite imagery- nor'easter of April 16, 2007 (photo: NOAA-NASA GOES Project). E, Satellite imagery- nor'easter of November 12-14, 2009; "Nor'easter Ida" (photo: NOAA-NASA GOES Project). F, Satellite imagery- nor'easter of December 18-19, 2009; "Blizzard of 2009" (photo: NOAA-NASA GOES Project). G, Satellite imagery- nor'easter of February 6, 2010 (photo: NOAA-NASA GOES Project).

www.ingramcontent.com/pod-product-compliance
Lightning Source LLC
Chambersburg PA
CBHW080427290526
45791CB00008BA/2422